TAMANA:
At Home in Africa

Patricia McGregor

TAMANA: At Home in Africa
by Patricia McGregor

Printed in the United States of America

ISBN 9781625096999

www.xulonpress.com

TABLE OF CONTENTS

Tamana is dedicated to my neighbors in Ankilifaly
and others living in impoverished environments
all over the world.

FOREWARD

*P*atsy spoke to us, as we gathered as bishops' spouses at the 2008 Lambeth Conference in Canterbury, England. She spoke, with tears running down her face, of God's call to her husband, Todd, to return to Madagascar as a bishop. God's call to Todd was, inevitably, a call to Patsy, too. But Patsy couldn't see what she would have to offer God, until God reminded her of the story of the widow's mite. Patsy was to offer whatever she had, however inadequate it felt, and God would know its value and how to use it.

Tamana describes how Patsy came to be just where God needed her and her gifts. But also how, in the generous, humourous love of God, Patsy realised that she was being given what she needed, as she offered what she had.

Patsy describes the poverty, the illness, the sheer effort of life in Madagascar without sentiment. But she also describes the riches of love, interdependence and community.

God may not be calling all of us to Madagascar, but he is calling all of us to be missionaries, that is, to be people who witness to the love of the God who came to make his home with us, so that we may find our own true homes, our *Tamana*.

Dr. Jane Williams

Tutor in Theology at St. Mellitus College,

London and Chelmsford

Wife of the former Archbishop of Canterbury

ACKNOWLEDGEMENTS

"*I am because we are.*" *The well-known statement by African theologian John Mbiti holds true in the writing of this book. We have been a team; there are many people who have helped put words into print. I would like to thank: Peg Hess, Howard Hess, Polly Montgomery, Pat Wright, Ryan Brazille, and Jane Williams for their invaluable feedback, ideas, and editing. I am also grateful to Peg Hess, who took the majority of photographs that illustrate this book.*

I am deeply appreciative to the People Reaching People Board of Directors and to our faithful mission partners who continue to bless us in more ways than words can express.

I am also truly grateful both for my family and to them for holding my hand as we continue our journey together: Todd McGregor, Charese

McGregor, Corbi McGregor Sandoe, Joe Sandoe, Audrey Cox, Gerry Cox, and the Wenzel family.

In addition, I am indebted to my friends in Ankilifaly and the Malagasy Episcopal Church who have taught me love, compassion, and what it means to live together in community. Most of all, I thank God, who promises that those who seek will find. As a result, I have found Tamana.

PREFACE

*T*amana is the Malagasy word for "happily settled; liking a place or a situation." *Tamana* encompasses our four years of missionary experiences in Toliara, Madagascar. Through much frustration my husband, Todd, and I worked on building a permanent home here in Toliara, called The Gathering Place. At the same time I was experiencing frustration in my personal journey of making Toliara home in my heart. I wrote this book as a set of reflections on what has been a dramatically different life for a middle-class American woman living with her husband in a slum in one of the world's poorest countries.

Tamana is written as an inspirational book that describes my experience of learning to be content wherever God places me in this world. For me, in this specific story, that situation meant to be settled as a bishop's wife in poverty-stricken Toliara, where *seventy percent* of the people live without water or electricity. Ankilifaly, the neighborhood where we lived while waiting for the completion of The Gathering Place, is a small section of Toliara, a port city on the southwestern coast of Madagascar.

Patsy and Todd in Toliara

The book draws upon my journals, reflections from the windows of our residence, conversations with others, *The Book of Common Prayer*, and other resources I relied upon during that experience, such as *The Celtic Way of Evangelism* by George G. Hunter. Each chapter focuses on one of the six themes from the Celtic method: go to the people, live among them, learn from them, love them, start with what they know, and build on what they have.

I hope *Tamana* will enable Christians to more fully realize their ability and responsibility to take part in carrying out the Great Commission as we endeavor to love the Lord our God with all our heart, body, soul, and mind, and to love our neighbors as ourselves. It is my prayer and hope that *Tamana* will also encourage others to reflect upon their own life circumstances and to more fully learn to be content—even to rejoice—in all circumstances.

To facilitate readers' reflections about their own spiritual journeys and challenges, I have concluded each chapter with "Opportunities for Personal Reflection." These concluding sections highlight experiences that are described in the chapter and suggest questions for careful thought, reflection, and prayer concerning both the chapter theme (i.e., go to the people) and the reader's own spiritual growth. Opportunities for Personal Reflection may be used to guide individual exploration and discovery as well as to structure and focus small group discussion.

The apostle Paul wrote from prison that he was able to be content in whatever state he found himself. I struggled, and still continue to struggle, to learn that lesson. Especially in Toliara, I often found the practicality of daily life in a slum to be overwhelming. I am prone to pride and selfishness. As you will see, I faced as never before the distance between my life previously and the lives of my new neighbors.

I do not try to hide my struggles from the reader. However, I believe my story to be one of hope and healing and, as I have already said, finding home. So alongside fear and mistrust, I hope you are able to see strength and endurance that can only be found in our Savior, Jesus Christ.

I am not the main character in this story, God is. My prayer is that he would shine through my story and make it beautiful, as he is beautiful. And my prayer is that, through reading this, you would find greater courage to believe that God wants to tell his story through your life as well.

I could never have imagined or planned my story. Had I tried, it would have been, quite literally, thousands of miles away from what actually took place. After all, people rarely choose to live in the midst of poverty and deprivation if they can avoid it. However, in retrospect, I strongly believe being a missionary was God's plan for me from before I was born. So I am learning to live into my calling, as in Ephesians 4:1: "I beg you to lead a life worthy of your calling, for you have been called by God."

No, God has not given me the story I wanted. And thank goodness! My wants can be so small and silly. Instead, he has given me something better. He has given me more than I could ever have possibly wanted. He has given me the precious gifts that I never knew to ask for, and more than I could ever have possibly wanted. He has given me love, joy, and community. He has given me *Tamana*.

Madagascar map

WHERE I, PATSY, AM FROM[1]

It was never a dream of mine to become a missionary.

It wasn't in my life-long strategic plan.

It wasn't on my bucket list.

It was never a dream of mine to move to Madagascar

in 1991, raising my daughters in the capital of

one of the world's poorest countries.

It was never a dream of mine to start all over again

in Kenya in 2002, with children in boarding school and

a husband who flew by small chartered missionary flights,

spreading the gospel while protected by armed guards.

It was never a dream of mine to leave

Kenya, my daughters, and my ministry at St. Julian's

in order to follow my husband back to Madagascar

in 2007, into the slums of Toliara.

It was never a dream of mine to live in a small

cement "box" for three years.

And, it was never my dream to leave home,

after home, after home.

---

[1] This poem and other "Where I'm From" poems in this book are based on the work of George Ellen Lyon, in *Where I'm From, Writers' & Young Writers' Series 2*, 1st ed. (New York: Absey & Co., 1999).

Yet, the words of John Wesley rang true when he said

that we should not only go to those who want us,

but to those who need us the most.

It *was* God's dream.

God was making for me a home that I would

never have to leave.

God was making his home in me.

TAMANA

PART ONE: GO TO THE PEOPLE

'Will you proclaim by word and example the Good News of God in
Christ? I will, with God's help.'[2]

TODD'S WINDOW

"Come on, Patsy, Let's Go!"

"**Y**ou're not going to do *that*, are you?" I asked my husband, Todd. I was stunned. I was shocked. I was in disbelief. In 1992 Dr. Zoe was the first doctor Todd hired to run the dispensaries in Antananarivo (Tana), the capital of Madagascar. She had been talking with the Bishop of Antananarivo about candidates for the position of assistant

---

[2] *The Book of Common Prayer* (New York: Seabury Press, 1979), 305.

bishop of Antananarivo and missionary bishop of Toliara. During the conversation, Todd's name came up as good candidate. Dr. Zoe emailed Todd to ask that he consider going back to serve the Malagasy people as Bishop of Toliara, the southwestern region of Madagascar. Now Todd was proposing that we—he and I—undertake this extremely difficult and daunting task. I knew the cost. I knew the sacrifice. Prior to our four and a half year stay in Kenya, we had spent eleven tough and trying years as missionaries in Tana. From my perspective, living in Toliara would be an even greater sacrifice. The thought more than unsettled my quiet heart.

The words, "Come on, Patsy, let's go!" brought back memories from years earlier when Todd had asked me to be his wife. From the beginning of our relationship, I doubted whether I could follow Todd as his wife. I knew I loved him deeply, but I also knew God was calling Todd to go to places I did not believe I could go and to do things I did not believe I could do. His question was not just, "Will you marry me?" He was asking, "Will you *go* with me?" On the day that he proposed, Todd had surprised me by coming to the office where I was working as office manager for the International Women's Tennis Association. As he knocked on the glass window outside my office, he wore a huge grin and held a bouquet of roses. "Come on, Patsy, let's go!" he mouthed through the windowpane. I was shocked to see Todd at my workplace because it was an hour's drive from the church where he was working, and I was further surprised to have him ask me to leave work in the middle of the day. I quickly motioned for him to come to the front door, mouthing in reply, "I can't go *now!* We have a tennis tournament to run. I have a press release to get out!"

He repeated his invitation: "Come on, Patsy, let's go!"

"*What is he doing?*" I thought as I turned to my boss, Peachy. "Umm, Peachy…Todd's here and I…"

"I know. Go ahead. Go with him."

"You know? How do you know?"

"He called me this morning. Go ahead, Patsy. Go with him. Have *fun!*"

From the very beginning, Todd took me by surprise. "Come on, let's go." I had hesitated: "I can't go with you *now.*" Likewise, how often do we also doubt our call from God? The call is simple, but that does not make it any easier. God offers his hand for us to grasp and hold, just as this young man was offering his hand to me. "Come on, let's go!"

Go. A simple word. A simple action. But fear can be simply paralyzing.

Responding to God's Call to Toliara, Madagascar

But that was a marriage proposal. This Toliara proposal seemed to me to be an entirely different matter. Getting to the point of willingness to move back to Madagascar in 2007 required much soul searching and prayer. The year leading up to the move was a hard one. In August, 2006, I did not see God with a joyful grin and a beckoning twinkle in his eye. No, I felt totally abandoned by the Lord as I tried to integrate the news that we were headed back to Madagascar. I knew it would be a hard life there. Just thinking about it made me tired and weary. I knew that going to Toliara was the will of God, but it was a country with many complicated challenges. I found myself deeply resisting the effort and losses that I knew the move from Kenya would require.

But this upcoming journey was inevitable. I was going to *go*. On one hand, I was thrilled that my husband Todd was elected as the Assistant Bishop of Antananarivo in order to start a missionary diocese in Toliara. The Malagasy people loved Todd and highly respected his leadership skills. It was a great honor. Having lived in the capital of Madagascar for eleven years, we had developed friendships that would go a long way toward supporting our adjustment and ministry. I could not deny that his fit as bishop would be perfect. But I knew the transition would not be an easy one. On top of the challenging living conditions and the stresses of starting a new diocese in such a poor country, the diocese of Antananarivo did not yet accept women functioning as priests. I would not be able to fulfill my call to ordination, which I had just pursued in Kenya. Like the front windshield immediately following a tragic auto accident, I was shattered.

Letters from Toliara

Even before I went, the exact cost of *going* became much more evident. Todd left before the rest of our family and moved to Toliara in January, 2007. When he arrived, there was only a shell of an Anglican Church building. A cement block structure, the walls were four meters in height and there was not yet a roof. He was installed in a Roman Catholic theater with three clergy and five evangelists, who would serve as co-workers in an area the size of Florida. There was only one paved road. His letters to us his family didn't necessarily help.

Gray clouds were forming over my head...

Ten days ago, the students at the university went on strike because there was no electricity at school. The only reason I am able to write now is because the electricity came on early tonight, at 9:00 p.m. rather than at 10:00 p.m. Electricity has been out for over three weeks now during the day and comes on from 10:00 p.m. to 5:00 am...

The looming clouds overhead darkened...

The students were not alone in their strike. One Member of Parliament and a few other dignitaries also went on strike. The government said they would arrest people if they continued and it was peaceful on Thursday. However, Friday, they decided to strike again, and others gathered. As a result, it worsened and people started attacking and looting the shops. Most of this literally happened right in front of the church property. When the riot police and military arrived, they began to shoot up in the air. Some shot at the looters. Many looters scurried into the half-built church below our apartment and dropped their items, running up our stairs to our apartment to hide. Thankfully, it was locked and they had to run back down. There were so many of them they broke the railing...

It thundered in the black distance and started to sprinkle...

The next day the government arrested one Member of Parliament and a few other politicians, who remain in prison. On Saturday some of the students kidnapped the person in charge of the prison and demanded that the four people arrested be released from prison, but the govern-

ment never gave way. I am not sure what happened to the
head person responsible for the prison...

And now there was no stopping the downpour...

Things seem to be peaceful at this point. The trial for
the four in prison begins on Tuesday. There are at least
25 others in prison and 15 or so in the hospital. There
are about 25 shops which no longer exist but are like a
skeleton.
As you can see life is normal for me! I begin training
for the five evangelists, three priests, and eight catechists
tomorrow.
The service went well this morning and everybody was
happy to see me. Well, that's about all for now...
I love you all, Daddy."[5]

My life was in the middle of a torrential flood.

An Interlude in America

As we prepared to move to Toliara, God gave me just
enough strength to face each stormy day. Looking back, I can
see how God was preparing me for the return to Madagascar.
He knew exactly what I needed, and I found help and clarifica-
tion as Todd and I studied for our doctorates. In June 2007,
Todd and I flew to Charlotte, North Carolina, to study for

---

[5] Todd McGregor, e-mail to author, Sunday, May 6, 2007.

our Doctorate of Ministry degree through Gordon-Conwell Theological Seminary. It was the first of three summer residential programs, and I found it inspiring to sit next to my husband, to learn together, and to chisel out our ministry dreams and goals for the future—a future that would now be in Toliara

We had been asked by Dr. Robert Coleman, author of *The Master Plan of Evangelism,* to be part of this program when he and his wife Marietta came to Kenya in September of 2006. What an honor it had been to host Dr. Coleman at our ministry site in Kenya, St. Julian's Centre and have him and Marietta at my ordination into the priesthood on September 3, 2006! He was like a Christian guru to Todd. Todd had wanted to take some of his classes while the two of us had studied for our Masters Degrees (1986-1990) at Trinity Evangelical Divinity School in Deerfield, IL. However, Dr. Coleman would only accept twelve students per term, counting them as disciples and teaching that the example Christ gave us was the one we were to model in ministry. When he gave us the opportunity to study under his tutelage, we both knew it was an opportunity we didn't want to pass up. The purpose of the program was to equip us for ministry in the areas of outreach and discipleship, specifically carving into the program our personal call and passions in ministry.

Facing an imminent move to Toliara, Todd and I were obviously at a pivotal point in our lives as we went through this program. It was a gift to have this time to redefine and work through what God would have us do. God had been doing such a great thing in Northern Kenya (2004-2006), and even before that in Madagascar when we lived in the capital, Tana (1991-2002). We were yet again totally dependent on his revealing his way to us so that we might not be led astray.

As Todd and I looked ahead, we knew we had many ministry needs and tasks related to building a diocese from scratch, including building a multipurpose training center, a dormitory, a guesthouse, the bishop's house, many churches, and a cathedral. We were fund-raising for all the structural needs of a diocese in one of the poorest countries of the world. Yet Todd himself had no salary, no staff, no office, and no church, and he was surrounded by the tremendous needs of the Malagasy people. It was overwhelming.

There were also longer-range ministry dreams. There was the possibility to build a beachfront hotel for economic development and to raise the local standard of living by providing jobs for the Malagasy people. On my flight back from our first year of Doctorate of Ministry classes, I had the very strong impression that the Lord really was going to cause this to happen. Tears began to flow down my cheeks. I had such a strong sense that the ultimate Dream Giver—the one who caused the dream of the boutique beach hotel to be in my heart in the first place—would cause his will to be done on earth as it is in heaven. As long as we are walking in his will, he will cause all these things to come about.

I remembered the Scripture from 2 Timothy 1:7, "For God has not given us a spirit of fear, but of power and of love and of a sound mind." When I thought about the wisdom and scope of God's plan, I fell to my knees, shouting, "Abba, Father."

God was being faithful to his promise. Step by step he was leading me on the journey to Toliara, and I was so thankful for this "step" of doctoral studies in North Carolina. I was walking alone, but the best guide and friend was going with me. Was the journey over? No, it was just beginning. But amidst the storm and tumult of my heart, the brilliant light of God's truth and goodness had broken through the heavy clouds. It was the hope I needed until the next stormy season.

Preparing to Go

After our first residency in North Carolina, I went to Kenya to begin bringing closure to my ministry at St. Julian's Centre. Todd returned alone to southern Madagascar, where thousands had never heard of Jesus before. He, the three clergy, and five evangelists covered a thousand miles of coastland from north of Morondava all the way south and then east to Ft. Dauphin, doing an evangelistic crusade. They visited hut-to-hut, telling people about the good news of the Lord Jesus Christ and showing the Campus Crusade Jesus film in the local Malagasy language.

Todd then returned to Kenya where we together attended our older daughter Corbi's graduation from Rift Valley Academy, the international school where the girls boarded, before moving permanently to Toliara. This graduation heralded an additional difficulty to the incoming seasons of life.

Preparing to Go: The "Empty Nest"

As we prepared for the challenges and (hopefully) blessings of new ministry, we also prepared for both of our daughters—first Corbi, then Charese—to begin college in the United

States. When most parents say that one of their children lives eight hours away, they are referring to driving distance. For me, "eight hours away" would be the difference in *time zones*. It was almost unbelievable that I would be *10,000 miles* away from my beloved girls.

As I packed on Corbi's bed in her dormitory at Rift Valley Academy, I had the stark realization that neither Corbi nor her younger sister Charese would be moving with us into this next stage of life in Toliara. They would each have their own stages to move into—college, jobs, marriage, children, and future goals. I wrote my reflections about these changes on a tear-stained journal, but I also realized how fortunate we had been to be so close in proximity and in relationship to the girls during their schooling at Rift Valley Academy. St. Julian's Center was only a forty-minute drive from the school. At a moment's notice, Todd and I could hop in the car and go visit the girls. The inviting and hospitable teachers and staff would even allow us to spend the night unexpectedly.

As I put duct tape and bubble wrap over a clay vase hand-made by Corbi, I pondered our blessings and once again thanked the Lord for leading us on the path to Kenya. The Lord had allowed us to be together for four years as a family and had used that time to unify our hearts and minds. The girls and I had become friends, very close friends in fact. Although I had not made these changes perfectly, I could see that I had transitioned from being my daughters' "overseer and nagger" to their "helper and encourager." So my journal in the summer of 2007 contained tears of a mother's heart, but that was ok. I needed to shed those tears. A part of me trusted God with what he was doing in our lives, but still I was truly feeling the empty nest.

We were all being called to *go*, but why did we have to *go* in such different directions? My family was being pulled apart and would soon scatter to four parts of the world. Corbi would be at college in America, Charese would be finishing high school in Kenya, Todd would be starting the ministry in Madagascar, and I would travel to all three destinations, trying to keep the family jigsaw puzzle pieced together.

It caused us all to ask the question, "Where *is* home?" In light of all these changes in our family, there was nothing to do but pray. I prayed that I would see things differently and that my heart would be flooded with light. I continually prayed that God would give us mighty inner strength through the Holy Spirit. I prayed that Christ would be more and more *at home* in our hearts as we trusted in him. With God's mighty power at work within us, he would be able to accomplish infinitely more than we would ever dare to ask or hope. I prayed that our roots would go down deep into the soil of God's marvelous love—that we might have the power to understand, as all God's people should, how wide, how long, how high and how deep his love really is. Finally, I prayed that we would experience the love of Christ, though it is so great we will never fully understand it. Then we will be filled with the fullness of life and power that comes from God.[6]

"God, What Is My Purpose?"

Another issue worried my mind as I prepared to officially move to Toliara in November, 2007. When I sought Christ, my main question was "What is my purpose?" That was my pivotal concern, "God, if I am going to *go* I would love to know *why* I'm going. What am I going to DO in Toliara?" I had just been ordained and saw my purpose, just to have it taken away from me.

I wondered, "What had made me feel at home in Kenya?" Maybe it was that I seemed to have my dream. I was developing my passion. St. Julian's Centre could not only be a retreat and conference center, but also a training center ground to

---

[6] Ephesians 3:14-20.

prepare new missionaries as well as to equip the local body of Christ in the Anglican Church of Kenya. I thrived in my new role as priest and greatly enjoyed leading the small congregation at St. Julian's Chapel. Not to mention, I was comfortable! I could be hostess in a beautiful environment. There were roses and a multitude of other flowers and birds to minister not only to the souls of those who came to St. Julian's Centre, but to my soul as well.

My husband was also happy. He was using his gifts and passions as a missionary in the desert regions of Northern Kenya, flying with Mission Aviation Fellowship to Marsabit. He had been modeling to others the importance of taking up their cross and following Christ wherever we are called in this world. When he was not traveling, Todd was teaching at St. Paul's University, just down the road from St. Julian's. I thought I was in the Land of Promise. So when God called us to walk together in another direction, back to Madagascar, I questioned. It seemed to me like a one-hundred-eighty-degree turn in the opposite direction—the *wrong* direction.

My dialogue with the Lord became somewhat of a one-way shouting match:

"Why Lord? Why back to the land of inconvenience and suffering? Why back to more hardships and difficulty? Why not stay here? We are happy! We are doing good works! Certainly not, Lord! I am just not strong enough. I don't want to go… and most certainly, nobody will come visit us there. It's the forgotten island."

"But trust me, this is your dream," the Dream Giver said.

"No, it's not!" I argued. "I found my dream at St. Julian's Centre. That was it! Why walk any further? I am tired, weary, and I want to rest. I want to stop and set down roots. What could you possibly have for me to do in the forgotten part of the forgotten island?"

"Choose to go on," the Dream Giver encouraged. "I will give you strength—food enough for the day and water, when you need to drink. I will give you a path to follow that leads to faith. My gracious favor is all you need. My power works best in your weakness."[7] And after days of wandering and wondering, I could finally respond, "To you, O Lord, I lift up my soul. I trust in you, my God"[8]. "Not as I will, but as you will."[9]

That response, "Your will be done," was the only way I could keep it all together. I was reminded of a powerful truth by Oswald Chambers: "The goal of the missionary is to do God's will, not to be useful or to win the lost. A missionary *is*

---

[7] 2 Corinthians 12:9 (New Living Translation).

[8] Psalm 25:1-2.

[9] Matthew 26:39.

useful and he *does* win the lost, but that is not his goal. *His goal is to do the will of his Lord.*"[10]

Times of Doubt

In the midst of embracing our call it is not uncommon to experience times of doubt and frustration. My insecurities were portrayed in a dream about a traffic jam. In the dream, I was rushing, trying to catch a flight in the capital of Madagascar, and was caught in a traffic jam. Frustrated and stuck, there was no way around the blockage on the narrow, windy, uphill roads of Antananarivo. Fidgeting in the taxi, I was losing patience because I knew the way. I could navigate myself to the airport, yet I was at a standstill, in the midst of it all. I could get out of the taxi and walk, but it wouldn't help. The distance was too far and would take too long, exhausting me on the journey. It was out of my control, so I needed to surrender. While sitting deadlock in the taxi, I then realized Todd was still in the capital and I was traveling before him, so what did it matter anyway? Isn't it better that we go together? Therefore, I re-booked the ticket, even though it was an extra cost, to go later with him.

---

[10] Oswald Chambers, *My Utmost for His Highest*, ed. James Reimann (Grand Rapids: Discovery House, 1992), *September 23.* (emphasis mine)

God used that dream to speak to me about use of my spiritual gifts in Madagascar, specifically in relation to women's ordination. Although the Province of the Indian Ocean had approved women's ordination into the priesthood in 2006, and women deacons were already being ordained in other parts of the Province, the Diocese of Antananarivo was not yet allowing women's ordination. At times I would get quite disappointed as I watched hungry believers sit through a Sunday morning prayer service, denied the opportunity to receive the body and blood of Christ through Eucharist because there were not enough priests to serve all the churches. And there I sat in the pew, desiring to be serving as a priest, but unable. My heart hurt with compassion, and I wanted to give the body of Christ to the people. Instead, I was caught in a traffic jam and even though it required an extra cost of self-sacrifice and humility, I needed to give up control, and go with Todd. Not before him, but with him.

A Hand Holder

I continued to struggle with what was God's will for me? A journal entry reflects God's reply to the question: "What is *my* purpose?" The blue fountain pen went to work:

I have been seeking the Lord about our return to Madagascar. It's scary, but I am ready. People ask me, 'What I am going to do?' I don't really know. I don't seem to have an answer. This morning I have again asked the Lord: 'What is my purpose?' He hasn't given me a title or a position, but I feel He has spoken to my heart. I am to be a hand holder. Many times in this world we are too busy to be a hand holder. On our journey of life we may stop on the road to shake someone's hand, but we are too busy, self-focused, worried or insecure to stop and hold that hand. Lord, teach me to be a hand-holder. Teach me to love Your people as You have created them, as they are Your sons and daughters.

A HAND-HOLDER

By Patsy McGregor

People ask me, "What do you do?"

I try to think of something impressive—in the world's view.

Nothing comes to mind and I humbly say

"I try to love people—in the Lord's way."

"I'm sorry," they reply, "You didn't hear what I said."

They don't understand—"What do you do?"

is the question I dread.

"Not really anything," again was my reply

As I took a deep breath and let out a long sigh.

"I try to love people—in the Lord's way."

But the world is not impressed,

as this doesn't take in much pay.

They want to know—what do I *really* do?

Rather than love one another and walk in one's shoes.

"A hand-holder"--that's my answer--that's what

I am called to be.

This goal is not impressive for others to see

But if the Lord were here at our side today,

It may be the answer he would say,

"Be a hand-holder" for the young and the old,

The simple, the elegant, the rich, and the poor.

These are children of mine—I've created each race—

Hold their hands and walk at their pace."

I prayed. "Teach me to do your will, for you are my God. May your gracious Spirit lead me forward on a firm footing."[11] Sometimes following the will of our Lord and Savior Jesus Christ is a learned response, just as we learn to listen to our spouse and children more carefully or learn a specific skill. Following Christ's will for us is a learned action, not the one we would do naturally. I had to learn once again to ask not, "What

---

[11] Psalm 143:10 (New Living Translation).

is *my* purpose?" a question with *me* at the center, but rather to ask, "God, what is *your purpose* for me?" a question that places *God* at the center.

Mary, the soon-to-be mother of Jesus took a great risk by submitting to the Father when she said, "May it be to me as you have said." Both her personal safety and reputation were in the balance. The scriptures are full of the stories of men and women of God whose lives and reputations were given over to God out of obedience to his call upon them. Submitting to the will of God subjects us to vulnerability. That's unnerving. We would rather be in control, but Christ desires vulnerability. Giving up control is a response that we can and must learn, but to learn to give up control we need to ask God to help us be obedient while trusting in Him and being available to God's will.

Two Copper Coins

One morning, I was given another helpful revelation to the question, "God, what is your purpose for me?" I heard the rooster crow, and I rose at 4:30 a.m. with the sun. Everyone was sleeping. It was the day of Todd's consecration as Assistant Bishop of Antananarivo to aid in the creation of the future diocese of Toliara. I grabbed my Bible and tiptoed out of our bedroom. Reading Jesus' parable about the widow who had only two small coins, I reflected that two small coins were all I had to offer the Lord. Tears ran down my cheeks. My husband was being consecrated bishop and would be going to Toliara, Madagascar, with all that was in him—dreams, goals, passion and excitement. I didn't have any of those to offer—just a hand to hold. I didn't have anything to give. I, like the widow, had only two very small copper coins, hardly worth anything. Symbolically, I put these two coins in my hand and lifted them up to God: *"Lord, I do not have much, but I do have these two, very small coins. What I do have, I give to you."* I believe that offering up and surrendering of myself to God's will was my personal consecration for the work ahead.

Called to Proclaim

It was prophetic. At the 2008 Lambeth Conference, a meeting held every ten years in Canterbury, England, for the purpose of gathering the worldwide bishops and spouses from the Anglican Communion, I somehow knew I was called to tell my story of the widow's mite. I believed I needed to be ready to speak with an open, honest, transparent heart and voice, to be vulnerable to the spouses of other bishops, and to share my struggle of loving the Lord God with all my heart, soul, and mind, and loving my neighbor as myself, especially since that neighbor was now in the slum of one of the poorest areas in one of the poorest countries in the world.

As I was waiting in the lunch line, a journalist randomly picked me out of the crowd and began to ask me questions about my ministry, my calling and my life as a bishop's spouse. It was then that I felt called to share the story of the two copper coins. A few days following[12] I was asked to speak at the afternoon plenary session at the Bishops' Spouses' Conference. To an elect group of church leaders, I humbly shared my story of the widow's mite. Two coins. Two copper coins. That was all I had to offer the second time going back to Madagascar. I had asked God, "Aren't my first eleven years of sacrificial service in Madagascar sufficient?" I had forfeited, served, and even grown in character, almost calling Madagascar home. But the Lord then called us to Kenya where I found missionary life could still be worthwhile but an easier, more comfortable experience. I could partner with my husband in vibrant ministry, a ministry that required much less sacrifice, especially in terms of language learning, personal discomfort, and the level

---

[12] July 24, 2008.

of poverty among the people. Wasn't missionary service to any country enough? Was the Lord truly calling us to another long period of hard sacrifice in Madagascar? The answer was emphatic: "Yes, he is."

Over five hundred people sat in small groups at round tables in the auditorium at the University of Kent and I shared my story of being called by God to "Go to the people" in Toliara and my deep resistance to God's call to go. I shared out of my weakness. It was hard. I cried—at the pulpit no less! I struggled to speak through my tears. But that is what God calls us to do. And I realized I wasn't the only bishop's spouse who struggled with following God. Many wiped their tears. I recounted how on Todd's day of consecration as bishop, I had little energy or excitement to give to the Lord. Early that morning I had read the story of the widow's mite. She offered two coins. Two very small cooper coins, hardly worth anything. That's all I had to give to the Lord. I reflected on the sacrifice. With tears streaming down my face I expressed what I was called to leave behind:

- Our children, one of whom would remain in Kenya in boarding school and the other who would begin her university education half way around the world from us

46

- Todd's salary, pension, medical and health benefits, due to the policies of the National Episcopal Church, which doesn't support missionaries who serve as bishops.
- Deep friendships
- My role as an ordained priest and manager of St. Julian's Retreat and Conference Centre
- A comfortable living environment
- Speaking in English most of my day

I contrasted myself with my husband, who seemed to be able to offer bags of talent and passion. His spiritual and natural gifts fit his new role as bishop. He was excited to go back to Madagascar. My gifts, however, seemed to be only worth two small coins. But what I had, I offered to the Lord. I lifted my open hands above my head and prayed: "Although it is only two small coins, what I have, I offer you, O Lord."

In responding to God's call to "*Go*" to Toliara, Madagascar, I learned that the Lord doesn't expect us to give what we don't have. He doesn't want us to put on a mask, nor to pretend to give more than what is in our heart. But when we honestly give what we do have, however little that may be, he will, like in the parable of the five talents, take what we give to him and multiply it and use it to his glory.

God calls us again and again to *go to the people*. Everyone. Everywhere. We must learn to accept that what is important to God is our sacrificial obedience to him, not how much we personally may have to give to the people. When we are obedient, God then blesses and multiples what we do have to give.

Marriage, Mitres, and Being Myself

Jane Williams, wife of former Archbishop of Canterbury Rowan Williams, is greatly enlightened about the sacrifices of being married to a bishop, and an archbishop. For the 2008 Lambeth Conference, she compiled the book, *Marriage, Mitres and Being Myself*, containing the experiences of many bishops' spouses in the Anglican Communion. As a well-educated theologian, she illustrates the calling to be in the church in spite of the difficulties with bureaucracy, feelings of powerlessness in the face of major upheavals, and the frustration at the difficulties of balancing duty, marriage and time to be yourself. Yet the overall impression is of a richness of life and opportunity, of a sense of privilege and of grace to surmount challenges that none of the spouses had imagined or sought.[13]

---

[13] Jane Williams, *Marriage, Mitres and Being Myself*, (London: Speck Publishing, 2008), back cover.

Not a single one of the many contributors remembered a childhood desire to be married to a bishop, and at that time there were only eight couples in the world who were bishops married to priests.

> Very few of them actually married a bishop, or even a priest. Most of them would have expected and even preferred a different path in life. But all of them walk with God, and they know that God's road has many corners, and that it is just no good trying to see around them until you come to them...I think the life would be almost impossible without that sense of walking with God in obedience and hope.[14]

I learned from my brothers and sisters in the Anglican Communion. The bishops' spouses who contributed to Jane Williams' book wrote:

> [We agree] that God and the Church cannot be just our spouse's profession. We too, are called to be disciples and ministers of Christ, and to be members of his body, the Church. That is what keeps us going when the job seems impossible. But it does make for very mixed feelings, at times...for many of us, it is a complicated emotional and spiritual matter...many spouses do not feel that their Christian calling is primarily to be a bishop's wife, and, while they almost all support their husband's calling in a great variety

---

[14] Williams, *Marriage, Mitres*, 1.

of ways, they don't, in their heart of hearts, think of themselves as being defined by their husband's role. Living with being defined by a title that is not chosen and doesn't seem to fit well is not easy. But in that we are no different from so many of our Christian brothers and sisters. Many people are unsure about how exactly their work and their faith fit together. Many Christians long to hear their God calling them into full-time mission or ministry and instead sense that they are called to go on being Christians to the best of their ability where they are.[15]

The Office Window

I processed many of these thoughts, feelings, and questions after arriving in Toliara. I associated different seasons and different lessons with different parts of the small apartment into which Todd and I had moved. I would look out different windows at different views of the city, and pray and think and learn. When I thought about the season when I was called to *"Go,"* I thought about Todd's office window.

As I reflect upon Todd's office window, I realize that rarely was I in this room except to be with Todd or sit in my Grandma Rittenhouse's soft-cushioned rocking chair, the one luxury item that we had brought over to Madagascar fifteen years earlier. I

---

[15] Williams, *Marriage, Mitres*, 5-7.

would escape the hard benches and enjoy the cotton-like padding as I prayed in color[16], wrote emails on the blackberry and watched tennis or CNN. This was primarily Todd's space, his walk-in closet, where he wrote official office correspondence while he rotated from one role in life to another—bishop, husband, father, mentor, problem solver, peacemaker, friend and confidant. Careful not to be in his very small space too much, I did not peer for long moments out this window. If I had, it would have been quite disastrous with the strong Toliara wind blowing all over and off his desk.

Neighbor sitting on roof of building
across the street from Todd's window

---

[16] Often, I find that words cannot adequately communicate the groaning of my heart. I often find it very helpful to pour out my heart to God, and to listen to him as I draw and color. For further information about praying in color I suggest *Praying in Color*, (Paraclete Press, 2007) by Sybil MacBeth.

Our family was respectful of this room as Todd's, yet as we gathered over the Christmas holidays it was the room that would make the memories. With family photos displayed on the back of the dining room china cabinets (which served as one of the walls in Todd's room), it was the room where the girls shared recent happenings of their semester at college, giving insight into their challenging life as third culture kids.

Some windows do not belong to us. I've always had a goal to be the best wife and mother that I ever could be. Little did I realize this would mean following my husband to the mission field and having a variety of responsibilities, among them opening our home to our daughters' classmates and friends during mid-term breaks and weekends. I have always desired our home to be the hub, to be the life of the party, a place where one could come for refuge, rest and recreation. In many ways, our home at St. Julian's Centre provided just that. As a mother whose primary desire was to provide a loving, caring, peaceful environment for her family, I rejoiced that the girls felt comfortable to invite their friends to come home with them and to host class parties. We also hosted leadership weekends and Sunday school retreats.

And now I was mourning that loss. The Lord had taken us even further away—to a poverty-stricken, dirty, and desolate destination in a remote area where our home would be far less appealing or even accessible to visitors. But, once I was living in Toliara, I realized I did have a place to welcome a guest! Because of the remoteness of the destination, my home, a humble safe haven, would be even more appreciated by those who entered. We now had a bed and a place setting at the table to offer the weary soul. Because God had taken me so far away, I could provide a much needed home for many. Because I left the land of ordinary, the land of familiar, people had a home to visit in the land of the extraordinary, in the land of the unfamiliar—and that is one of the most appreciated places of all.

It would take much more time and many more lessons, but eventually I would learn to call Toliara home as well.

Bless You, Prison, for Being in My Life

The Soviet, Aleksandr Solzhenitsyn, looked back on the years he spent in the infamous Gulag, and declared, "Bless you, prison, for having been in my life. For there it was lying on rotten prison straw, that I learned that the meaning of earthly

existence lies not, as we have grown used to thinking, in pros-
pering, but in the development of the soul."[17]

The German pastor Dietrich Bonhoeffer also endured
soul-searching character-building during his time in prison.
During the Nazi regime of Adolf Hitler he wrote, "As I see it,
I am here for some purpose, and I only hope I may fulfill it. In
the light of the great purpose all our privations and disappoint-
ments are trivial."[18]

Many times as I was getting ready to leave Kenya (or the
United States) to go to Southern Madagascar, I also felt like I
was in a prison, hand-cuffed to a God calling me to, "*Go.*" Just
as I had to grapple with my own call and the views from my
windows during this somewhat nerve-wracking time, I learned
to embrace the difficulties.

When looking at the life of the biblical character Joseph,
humanly speaking, we think he had setback after setback. But,

> From God's point of view, he was being carefully pre-
> pared for his life's calling and destiny. We are often
> concerned about getting a task finished. God is con-
> cerned about getting the person prepared so that he
> or she can finish the task. We want a job done; God

---

[17] Aleksandr Solzhenitsyn, *The Gulag Archipelago, 1918-1956, Vol. 2* (New
York: Harper & Row, 1975), 617.

[18] Dietrich Bonhoeffer, *Letters and Papers from Prison*, May 9, 1944 letter,
(New York: Macmillan, 1953), 159.

wants a person molded. We want to work for God; God desires to work on us.[19]

God was working on me through Todd's call into mission.

As I continued to look deep into my heart, I realized that I was finding peace and, like dawn beginning to paint the eastern sky, a heartfelt joy to go back to Madagascar began to color my heart. I believed I was at a healthy place in my marriage as we walked back on a journey to Madagascar. I also sensed a calling and a responsibility to go back, glued together with a love for the people. After a struggle through the process, I could say that the Lord brought me to the point where I was truly willing to go back.

Learning Obedience

"Sometimes God calms the storm and sometimes he lets the storm rage and calms his child."[20] Jesus learned obedience through what he suffered.[21] Our spiritual lives are a process;

---

[19] David W.F. Wong, *Journeys Beyond the Comfort Zone*, (Singapore: BAC Printers, 2001), 28.

[20] Common quote. Original author unknown.

[21] Hebrews 5:8.

even Jesus' spiritual life was a process as he learned obedience. For the past seventeen years on the mission field, specifically the first eleven in Madagascar, I struggled because I continually thought that life must be easier than what I was experiencing. However, as we grow in the grace of God, we realize that the way of the cross is never easy. No matter where we are in the world, when we are chosen by Christ to do his work, the path will never be easy. If we have the false expectation that it should be, it could be the deceit of a camouflaged enemy bringing a spirit of dissatisfaction and discontentment to discourage and defeat us. Christ reveals to us the true suffering of the cross and the abundant life of joy in the midst of life's difficulties. This is the mysterious and wonderful truth of the gospel and serving our Lord.

To find that wonderful and difficult path of joy, I had to take the first step, and the first step was simply to go. First steps are huge and scary for an infant. I was realizing that, even after years of missionary service, I could still have fears like a child. From where would my peace come?

WHERE TODD IS FROM

He's from independence, family breakup, father and step-mom trying to put it all back together with children of yours, mine, and ours.

He's from a clan of ten where everybody lived
in one house, but did their own thing.
He learned never to ask for anything.
He's from the Green Mountains of Vermont,
lakeside town by Lake Champlain.
He's from working hard at the pharmacy with his dad, the
owner, trying to make ends meet with a large family to feed.
He's from Roman rosaries and catechisms turned into
an abundant life with Christ, ready to do the
Will of God wherever he be sent in the world.
He's from the high mountains of Nepal,
imprisoned by the Nepalese government.
He's from trekking hundreds of miles into the
Madagascar jungles with the Cross to find the
forgotten, where the village drunk,
who is now ordained, came to
faith in Christ.
He's from knives and machine guns,
surviving robberies and attacks, protecting
his family through it all.
He's from cattle dung and stick huts in the
Northern Kenyan bush where he served
as best man to a Kenyan brother in Christ.
He's from the semi-arid desert of Southern Madagascar
where churches had never been planted,
water had not been tapped, and the few people
who live there, live off the land.
He's from such comfort with the rainforest,
that even with his bishop's miter,
some call him Rainforest Man.
He's from seeking and finding, knocking
and opening, without questioning,
totally dependent on the Lord,
his God.

Woman in the market below Patsy and Todd's apartment

Malagsay man in the market below Patsy and Todd's apartment

Opportunities for Personal Reflection:

As described in the Preface, the following questions are intended to encourage and support readers' personal reflection. Space for notes is provided.

"He who deliberates fully before taking a step will spend his entire life on one leg."[22]

Has there been a time in your life when the Lord has called you to *go* out of your comfort zone? How did you respond? Was it your natural response or a learned response with a learned action as referred to in this chapter? Journal about a few ways that God has changed you through obedience.

On the day Todd proposed, we left my office and Todd blindfolded me. I had no idea where we were going or why, but I had perfect peace. I had peace because I trusted. Neither "Where?" nor "Why?" was the issue. Rather, the question was "who am I with and how does this relate to my journey with God?"

Has there been a time in your life when you followed somebody, including God, with blind faith? What was the outcome?

---

[22] Chinese Proverb.

Plaque hanging in dining room

TAMANA

PART TWO:
LIVE AMONG THEM

"Will you continue in the apostles' teaching and fellowship, in the breaking of bread, and in the prayers?" "I will, with God's help."[23]

THE DINING ROOM WINDOW

It's a Shock!

*I*mmediately after making the two-day exhausting drive from Tana, Charese, Todd, and I came straight to the house where we were to live temporarily until permanent housing for the bishop's family was completed. I hadn't seen the

---

[23] *The Book of Common Prayer*, 304.

house before. I remember driving up to the house and walking up the stairs for the first time to our second floor apartment, which I later nicknamed "the box." As I came up the stairs I felt uncertainty. We were surrounded by uncertainty—I was uncertain about the house and the neighborhood, the neighbors were uncertain about the new foreigners, and Todd may have been uncertain too, wondering how comfortable his wife would be living shoulder-to-shoulder with the people who lived next door to us, in a slum. Charese seemed to be uncertain, too. What were her parents doing moving into such a poverty-stricken area? She came home from boarding school to *this*?

Looking around, I could sense God asking a new question. I had followed God. I had gone. But now the Lord was asking even more, "*Will you live among them?*"

As I took each step, I could see people from the neighborhood staring up at us. One young woman, standing by the entrance of her tiny thrown-together shack called out, "*Salama*," (Hello). I saw another neighbor drinking dirty water from a bowl with a naked child sitting at her feet. She smiled at me. I didn't want to see anything else. I wanted to be blind for a while. *"Don't give me too much sight, please Lord."* That day, as I walked up the stairs to the second floor, I could only see the slum, not the smiles. I saw tin shacks and bamboo huts. I saw poverty, dirt, and grime. I saw outside public bathing areas and people freely going to the bathroom wherever they wanted. I saw the place, not the people, and the place seemed nightmarish to me. I was so thankful this was going to be temporary…

Three years later, a friend of mine, Peg Hess, came to Madagascar for two months with her husband while he was on sabbatical. We were still in our "temporary" housing. She knew she would be living with us for two weeks of their stay. She shared with me her reaction to coming up these same stairs and looking at the slum beyond. As Peg slowly walked up the stairs, she found herself praying, *"God, I don't think I can do this."* Her reaction brought back the memory of my own thoughts and feelings coming up those stairs. I, too, had told God that I didn't know how I would live here among the people. From the beginning, a part of me asked, "Why?" Another part of me was ready to leave.

First Impressions

When I walked into our apartment, I was somewhat pleasantly surprised. Between his installation as bishop almost a year earlier in January and my arrival in November, Todd had worked very hard to set up our small apartment well. Nothing is easy in Madagascar. The dining room table and several larger pieces of furniture had to be lifted onto the roof of the vicarage next door and carried by several men through the second-floor dining room window since they would not fit through the hallway or the front door. The rooms were very crowded, especially our bedroom. When Todd was setting up the room, he placed the queen-sized bed facing the opposite wall. However, he decided that I might like it the opposite way instead, to benefit from the direction of the incoming breeze. *The entire bed had to be taken apart to move it within the room.*

In order to get into my closet I had to slide sideways past the closet door and then open it half way to get my clothes out. The room was lit by a single light bulb, blocked by the closet door, which didn't allow any light to find the color combinations I was used to. Like fishing, I was not exactly sure what catch I would pull out of the closet. It was interesting to see what I sometimes pulled out. But it really didn't matter to my new neighbors, who wore the same thing day in and day out.

Stairs to "the box," Patsy and Todd's apartment

View from apartment landing: St Luke's Malagasy Episcopal Church on the right, Ankilifaly neighborhood to the left

View from apartment landing; Ankilifaly neighbors' homes

The kitchen was workable, but the doors to the apartment were so small that the refrigerator could not squeeze through and therefore was placed downstairs. If we wanted anything as simple as a glass of cold water, someone had to go outside, down the stairs, through the door downstairs and into another person's living space, and then into the room where our refrigerator was found.

Size aside, our apartment did have most of what we needed. One might even call it cozy. We had purchased some furniture, dishes, and kitchen utensils from missionaries that were leaving, and Todd had somehow gotten them from Tana to Toliara. Unlike all of our new neighbors, we had running water in the kitchen and bathroom. I quickly learned, however, that it was not running often, especially during the day! But we learned to work the system by placing a twenty-gallon trashcan next to the shower and filling it at night so we could always take a "bucket bath."

I wondered why God had us living here. Surely there was another option. Surely we could have found a place with more space and reliable running water. Todd was a bishop now, after all! But, as always, God did not answer all my questions and objections immediately.

I remember glancing dubiously out the windows through the open wooden shutters that first day, but I didn't study or observe the world outside the windows. I couldn't take it in. It was like being in a dark room; when I opened the shutters, my eyes couldn't adjust. The poverty was painful to see, the view too harsh. It took a long time for me to really absorb what I was seeing, both inside and outside the apartment. I learned I had to open my eyes little by little as I began to live among them.

After five days in Toliara, my mind felt cloudy. I didn't even have an idea of the date. I wrote in my journal:

> All I know is that last Thursday was Thanksgiving and now it is five days later. So it must be around the 27th of November. Not looking at a calendar is only one of the simplicities of life here. How about not wearing a watch or looking into a mirror? Life is no longer about what time it is or what we look like.

Moving In

Physically, it was fairly easy to move in; I had only one suitcase to unpack. Moving in emotionally was another matter. Out of every window was unrelenting poverty. Every time I went out our front door I would see the neighbors' latrine and shower space. It was not uncommon to see topless women sitting outside their homes, wearing a loose *lamba*[24] that would easily fall down so they could feed their children.

The windows of the apartment—one in each room—were covered with wooden shutters that opened and closed. With no glass or curtains in the windows, the inside of our apartment was visible to the whole neighborhood. Later, we hung curtains at each window. I now know that curtains soften the view, screen the flies, provide privacy, and keep it cooler. But here at the beginning there were no curtains, and it was just *hot*. Charese called it the "hot box" as it was rarely below ninety-two degrees in the summer months.

And our first months in Toliara were the summer months—December, January, and February. With the heat came summer's constant stench of sweat, burning charcoal, rotting garbage, and urine. In the market, there were smells of fish, fat, flesh, and organs. I watched from the windows and encapsulated thoughts in my journal.

---

[24] A piece of cloth worn by women as they cook outside.

View from Patsy and Todd's bedroom window

View of Patsy and Todd's bedroom
window from neighborhood below

Four neighbors are still sleeping outside on a grass mat, covered like a mummy from head to toe, keeping mosquitoes at bay. A few women glance and smile as I sit at the window on the edge of my bed peering into the slum below. They carry their day's water on their heads after lining up to draw it from the community tap. A drunken man stumbles by. I say a prayer and know God hears.

An older woman from the 'deluxe' bamboo hut below prepares her family's morning meal of vary sosoa (rice porridge watery rice). The reason I say 'deluxe' is because their hut has a tin roof on a portion of it, bettering the most common grass thatch. A woman carries her cooking pots from the bamboo hut where they are stored at night.

The sky is now a bright yellow where the sun will shine in a few minutes. A young man gets up off the grass mat. His friend rolls over for a few more winks, not yet ready to greet the day.

This is my neighborhood, my slum, where I live, reside and, hopefully, thrive. You have brought me here, Lord, to transform me—to go beyond the concept of being comfortable in body and causing me to strive to be comfortable in soul. You are causing me to learn from these neighbors…the naked little boy who incessantly waves hello, the teenage girl who nods, "Salama" (Hello) with her chin, the boy carrying his black half-filled charcoal sack, hoping to sell a few pieces for his day's wages.

It's a hard-knocked life. The song from the movie hit Annie comes to mind. These neighbors are poor, desperately poor. The woman dressed in a simple cloth gives last night's left-over rice to her chickens. But she seems happy, genuinely happy, such a dichotomy in today's western world. Happy, although poor, how can it be?[25]

"Happy, although poor?
How can it be?
For they have nothing
Compared to others, you see.
But they are a content, joy-filled, neighborhood and family.
Lord, please speak, what does this show me?"

I was beginning to see the first glimpses of why God had me living in Ankilifaly.

---

[25] March 6, 2008.

The Dining Room Window

The small dining room, furnished with a table around which sat four chairs, with two plastic ones added for company, was the hub of the house. From here I observed the life of the fifth largest city in Madagascar, a port city of 125,000 people. The road along this side of church was a marketplace. People, bicycles, *pousse-pousses* (rickshaws), cars and trucks were everywhere. I would observe rickshaw accidents and watch the aggressive culture of the South as they firmly spoke loudly to one another, at times watching a fistfight break out. From this window I would watch the military troops take their morning run in-step while chanting military songs.

Funeral procession passing below dining room window

Malagasy pous-pous on street below dining room window

It was from the dining room window that Todd and I watched the political coup.

We were not exposed from that window to the riots below. From there, people could not easily see our white and very out-of-place faces. We saw people running, carrying hundred-pound sacks of rice on their backs, stealing it from the local store or storage unit. During that arduous time of the political coup, our front door would be locked but the windows could be open in the dining room, bathroom, and Todd's office. However, the guest bedroom window could not be opened since it was too exposed to the main road. I remembered

Todd's letter from the year before describing earlier political unrest. When we first arrived in Ankilifaly, there was neither a church wall nor a gate, and the area was very vulnerable. During the coup in January, 2009, police asked permission to be stationed in the church as it was an excellent location to observe the events of the city. We agreed.

It was unclear whether the police army was loyal or divided. We saw big military trucks, and troops with lots of guns. We heard gunfire and grenades, and we were told by our neighbors to stay inside. Mercifully we never felt personally threatened. The s*haman* next-door became our friend and offered to surround our home with the youth of the community and protect us if needed.

I stayed in the house and wrote:

> My heart mourns for this nation. Just three days ago, Feb 7, 2009, approximately 30 people were killed in the capital of Antananarivo. They called it 'Black Saturday.' The opposition and the presidential armies were fighting. I guess the opposition tried to march into the presidential offices in Tana to overcome the current government, and the army protecting the President was ordered to shoot. Some call it an attempted coup. Yesterday and today the people are in a state of mourning. The atmosphere on the streets is tense, but calm. But rumor has it that there will be retaliation. The Toliara-based opposition wants to

overtake the current major government. The ethnic parties have also begun to fight. Rumors on the street say the Antandroy (ethnic group from the south) are going to retaliate by attacking the Merina (ethnic group from the highlands) here in Toliara. People in the south are quite frightened. All we can do is pray, pray for peace upon this land.

The dining room window became our local daily newspaper in living print. One day Todd and I watched the community catch a local thief running from the market. There was a massive crowd of people gathered. Finally the thief was caught in the graveyard. The community then chained and beat the thief, finally taking him to the police. It was unnerving to watch him being chained and beaten. I prayed for the Lord's mercy.

But the dining room was not just a place to watch the shocking daily events. The dining room was also the place from which our hospitality flowed. It was our "everything" room, where we invited the *shaman* and his wife to come up and share soda and cookies; where I discipled neighborhood women and Todd discipled his student evangelists. It was where the bishop would hold Tuesday team meetings, we would eat family meals, and host short-term missionaries. In the small corner we squeezed the Christmas tree, hanging onto traditions like our Christmas stockings hung on the dining room chairs. To some who entered, it was a palace. To me, it was a small box from which we interacted with the local and international community. It represented my call, that difficult call, to live among them.

Counting My Blessings

There were blessings as well as challenges in the initial weeks and months. Our first visitors arrived! Phil Cranell stayed six days, and our friends Randy Degler and Phil Johnson remained another five. Either poolside or over dinner at their hotel, we were able to discuss several issues for People Reaching People, our newly formed nonprofit organization designed to reach the poorest of the poor in Eastern Africa. At the same time, we were able to locate property and brainstorm a future site-plan for The Cathedral Complex. After looking at several pieces of land, we selected a long, rectangular piece close to the airport with a view of Tabletop Mountain. Pleasantries and conversations were enjoyed with friends around, and the visit was also helpful for decision-making as we sought the future and progressed with People Reaching People and the Malagasy community. Phil described the trip as "transformational," and we both cried when we said "Good-bye" at the airport.

In addition, we had the gift of our daughter Charese's company longer than expected. Since she attended Rift Valley Academy, a boarding school in Kenya for missionaries' children, we knew she would be with us in Toliara for the school holiday, from Thanksgiving through New Year's Eve. However, due to a political crisis in Kenya, Charese remained in Toliara for two more weeks, and flew back to Kenya when Corbi had to go back to Dickinson College in the United States. We sang and cooked with our neighbors, taught our housekeeper Jeannette how to make pizza, and talked as a family.

Jeannette and Pierre and their family at beach near Toliara

We also were blessed by our house's guard, Pierre. He had worked for us for several years in Tana and decided to work for us again, moving with his family to Toliara. Moving to Toliara was a huge adjustment for Pierre's family too. Living on the same property in Tana, we had become good friends, and had missed them while living in Kenya. Pierre's wife, Jeannette, had previously worked in a factory in Tana and now wanted to work for us as a housekeeper in Toliara. Jeannette is very smart and trustworthy, has a wonderful sense of humor, and is a hard worker. We were grateful that she wanted to work for our family. She came to Toliara in early December and began training with me as our housekeeper after Christmas. I sometimes had difficulty focusing on the blessings—all of us had things we had given up. But having their company and support was a blessing.

Grieving My Losses

Making this transition emotionally was complicated by my deep sense of significant loss: loss of my role as a newly ordained priest serving my first parish;[26] loss of my role as

---

[26] I had been ordained and had served as a priest in Kenya. However, the diocese in Madagascar did not permit women to serve as priests.

caregiver for our daughters, both of whom were in school in other countries—Charese in Kenya and Corbi in the United States; loss of my aspired job, offering hospitality as the manager of the peaceful and beautiful retreat center in Kenya; loss of ease in language and communication due to the different Southern Malagasy dialect; loss of a comfortable home; and loss of friends and familiarity in getting around from place to place.

I missed the frequent and predictably accessible contact with the overseas world. After a day of working with the unreliable internet connection, Todd would many times only be able to send two emails! One morning I tried to send an email to Charese and Corbi, and after one half-hour of trying, I finally gave up while shedding a tear.

It wasn't easy for my parents either, to have their daughter and son-in-law living in such harsh conditions. Mom openly admitted,

> It was really difficult living, unhealthy living, especially being there for such an extended period of time. I felt like they needed to be elsewhere, and that they would be more productive elsewhere. After experiencing living in 'the box' for a month ourselves with Todd and Patsy, I realized how extremely difficult it was to always have people knocking at the door, and to have relentless, overwhelming needs continually

presented by people for whom they cared. There was no peace and quiet. I realized how talented Patsy and Todd were to make 'the box' so livable with nothing. There was barely room to turn around, but despite all this, their neighbors and friends were kind and loving, as is Malagasy personality and custom.[27]

My dad agreed.

I wasn't happy about having my daughter living in a slum, but knowing Patsy and Todd, I understand it was probably the thing for them to do. You've got to be with the people instead of hovering above them, allowing them to work with you and get to know you.

When we went to visit Patsy and Todd, I didn't mind staying in 'the box.' I felt that we were very safe. We had a roof over our head, the bed was comfortable enough and I'm not that big on grand things. Of course, we were only there for a few weeks, maybe after a year I would have a different opinion. But for however long I would be in 'the box,' I would feel safe because Patsy and Todd cultivated the people very well. Their neighbors were all very nice.

I am glad they're out of there now. Four years was a long time. But I also think that Patsy and Todd have the ability and the will to put up with more inconveniences than a great many people, and they do it with very little complaining.[28]

---

[27] Audrey Rittenhouse Cox, July 22, 2011.

[28] Gerry White Cox, Jr., July 22, 2011.

I am thankful for my father's opinion about my amount of complaining. My husband may have had another perspective.

What Am I Supposed to *Do*?

The question still plagued me. The answer from God was always the same: just watch, just live. Thomas Merton writes that "a man has found his vocation when he stops thinking about how to live and just starts living."[29] I wanted to learn how to live.

The Malagasy dialect in Toliara was different than the one spoken in Tana; this made conversation and comprehension more difficult. In retrospect, I understand that my sense of isolation and solitude as I began to live among the people most likely made me more dependent upon God. I found God impressing upon me: "*Love me through these people. Learn to love yourself. I have called you by name. You are fearfully and wonderfully made.*" It wasn't like I had to do anything in order to please God. God does not want our secular and spiritual lives to be separated like oil and vinegar. I was learning to live out my calling as an intercessor and prayer warrior, discipler, and

---

[29] Thomas Merton. *Thoughts in Solitude* (New York: Farrar, Strauss, Giroux, 1999), p. 84.

bishop's wife, which could be done sitting in a church pew or whenever I looked out the window. God wants us to be involved in relational evangelism.

Mother Teresa had a "call within a call" to work among the least of these. She knew she had to leave the convent (Loreto) and consecrate herself to help the poor and live among them.[30] "In determining which work would be done, there was no planning at all. I headed the work in accordance to how I felt called by the people's sufferings. God made me see what he wanted me to do."[31] Mother Teresa is a model for all individuals to live out the calling we have each received from God.[32] Quite simply she chose to leave the life of the convent and live among the people she served. Wouldn't the world be different if more of us chose to do the same?

Culture Shock

Even though I had been a missionary on the field for sixteen years, I still experienced culture shock when I moved to Toliara. "Culture shock refers to feelings of personal stress,

---

[30] Her story is told in *Mother Teresa: In My Own Words*, Complied by Jose Luis Gonzalez-Balado (New York: Gramercy, 1997), IX.

[31] *Mother Teresa: In My Own Words*, X.

[32] Ephesians 4:1.

confusion, uncertainty, anxiety, irritability, possible depression and withdrawal that may affect people exposed to an alien culture."[33] I was in a brand new area and definitely out of my comfort zone. Like a person learning to focus binoculars for the first time, I was learning to adjust my lens. I emailed a story to a prayer warrior friend in the States who previously lived in Toliara and described my first-hand experiences of the subtle darkness surrounding and oppressing the city:

> Yesterday, I traveled by myself in a taxi-busse to the beach village of Madiorano to look at land for a micro-development project. I had no idea I was sitting next to a witchdoctor until I listened to the conversation going on around me. People began talking about their professions. Most were fisherman, or sold fish, but the woman right next to me said 'Ombiasa aho.' (I am a witchdoctor.)

We faced our first Christmas in Toliara in hundred-degree heat as the girls, home for school holiday, tried to cook an egg on the front porch. It found me wondering, "Where do I find all the ingredients to cook our holiday favorites?" Still trying to keep family traditions, we searched for ingredients for cinnamon buns, pecan pie, turkey and its trimmings. I deeply felt

---

[33] Scott Kirby, *Equipped for Adventure* (Birmingham: New Hope Publishers, 2006), 106.

the loss of the familiar. Watching our guard kill the turkey by hand, I questioned, *"Can I really relax in Madagascar with its heat, inconvenience, dire poverty, and needs?"* My answer was that by the grace of God, I could. I now can look back and understand that the empty emotional place I had entered was to provide time and space for deepening my relationship with God. At the time, however, I was unhappy, and those closest to me were noticing.

After my first month in Toliara, Corbi asked her dad if there was one thing that he would change about me, and if so, what would it be? Resistance shot into my bones like a frightened cat's hair stands upright when defensive. *"Wait a minute,"* I thought to myself, hearing the conversation from another room. *"Do I even want her to ask that question?"*

Todd thought a moment and then replied, "I would want her to be more happy."

Thinking it better to write than to speak, I penned in my journal: *"*More happy? In this place? Sure, I can be more happy. Get me out of this dump. Take me to another living environment other than a slum. Something that's pretty! Then I might become a little more happy!"

Two years later I reflected on Todd and Corbi's conversation:

At the time I had just begun the adjustment to living in the slum of Madagascar, the ninth poorest country in the world. My neighbors lived off .75 cents a day…there was no escape. My ten-step by seven-step house left little room for leisure. I could not even fully spread my arms and turn around without knocking something over. If I wanted to quench my thirst with a glass of cold water in the 96 degree heat (in the house!) I would have to go outside, down the stairs, through another family's living quarters and to the refrigerator. Yes, I was definitely experiencing culture shock. [34]

Too Worn Out for Words

I was so emotionally worn out that my writings no longer had the energy for long sentences and I switched to poems.

FADED

A worn out dish rag
A faded skirt with an unraveled hem
Have you ever felt like that?
Like the heat of the day has sucked out all the color,
pep and vigor
From the depth of your soul?

Nothing left? Like a used tea bag—
Used, re-used and re-used again?

---

[34] Patsy McGregor journal, January 16, 2009.

No matter how long I steep, there is nothing left.
I guess it's time to find a new tea bag.

MY TIDE IS OUT

We all have our seasons of life,
when the ways of the world press upon us
and we would rather go up to heaven and be with our
Savior than remain here on earth to
plow through the journey.

I am having a season like that.
Like the ocean's water, my tide is out.
High tide brings activity and rushing about in life.
But low tide is a quiet season,
a time to observe what is actually under the surface,
a time when the ocean's pull causes us
to be stretched out to the ocean's depth,
exposed on the ocean's floor.

Sometimes the sight is not pretty, exposing
dirty plastic bags caught beneath coral, ripped from
currents below.
Rusty bottles, rotted containers eaten away by sea creatures,
covered with barnacles, block the beauty of the reef below.

Such are the seasons of life.
the ebbs and flows
...the tides of life.

We are reminded that there is a time and season for everything,[35] a time when the tide is in, and a time when the tide is out. This was a season when my tide was out.

Patience

It was also a time to wait… It was time to wait for the three titles of the cathedral complex land in Andranomena. It was a time to wait for People Reaching People (PRP) board members to share the vision and come and see what God is doing in Madagascar. It was a time to wait for the beachfront hotel to take shape, and for me to find my place in this world. It was a time for me to wait for friends and mission teams to come and visit and for family members to be together again. My tide was out. It was my time to wait. I found myself holding back.

HOLDING BACK

I have been holding back.
With a good look inside
and a spirit of self-introspection,
I ask myself,
am I truly loving those around me
with my whole heart, soul, body and mind?

---

[35] Ecclesiastes 3.

A caution flag rises.

I think I've been holding back--
Afraid of totally surrendering my heart
and trusting those around me.

Most of all, this includes trusting God.

When Ruth Bell Graham was asked to describe her and her husband's separations due to his many travels, she portrayed it as "again and again, like a small death, the closing of a door. One learns to live with pain. One looks ahead—not back— never back."[36]

SOMETIME

Sometimes I just want to fit in.
Not stand out in a crowd.
Not be white in a brown-skinned culture.
Sometimes I wish I could just snap a finger
And speak the language without fail.

Someday my day will come.
I will be able to converse in heavenly languages
And have a new body without color limitations.

There, I will be at home.
Home with my father, praising Him

---

[36] Ruth Bell Graham, *Footprints of a Pilgrim* (Kansas City: Lillenas Drama, 2001), 76.

With a whole assembly of heavenly beings.

There I will fit in.
There, I will be one of the heavenly hosts
And there I will praise my God forever and ever.

Bloom Where You Are Planted. In a Sack of Cement?

One is never at a loss of things to see when observing the sights in Madagascar—something interesting is always bound to catch the eye. One day, while playing tennis, I saw a sack of cement on someone's tin roof, holding it in place during summer rains and wind. Growing out of that sack of cement was a patch of flowers.

I felt the Lord's quiet whisper. *"Bloom where you are planted."*

Identifying with the sack of cement on a tin roof, I questioned him in response.

"How can I blossom in my circumstances? In a place as hard as a sack of cement?"

But God who began a good work within us will continue his work until it is finally finished on that day when Christ Jesus comes back again.[37] Over time, I began to see anticipa-

---

[37] Philippians 1:6.

tions of life popping through the hard stone. A sprig became a branch. A bud became a blossom. There was no denying that living in Toliara was as hard as a flower blooming in a sack of cement. But with a heavy dose of hope and prayer, watered by the Word of God and the rays from God's Son glorified, I too, began to bloom where I was planted.

But the whole truth is even more amazing. As I lived among the people of Toliara, it was not just that I was able to bloom in a difficult place. It was that I was able to bloom and grow in ways I never could have had I *not* lived among the people. By the power of God, the "bag of cement" became the richest soil. Glory be to God![38]

Surrender and Sacrifice

For so many years I doubted myself on the mission field. Would I really be able to run the mission field marathon? Could Todd and I go the full distance, hand in hand, together? Was this a specifically tailored, custom-designed call on my life, intricately fashioned by the divine dressmaker himself, or

---

[38] Todd later commented that the sack was originally filled with cement but used and replaced with dirt. Nevertheless, knowing this did not diminish the effect of the lesson the Lord was teaching me.

a pre-cut-one-size-fits-all pattern to hastily slip on over the shoulders?

Four months after moving to Toliara, I still continued to wrestle with living among the people of Toliara. I journaled:[39]

> Good Morning Lord. This morning, mid-morning, I pause from the busy-ness of writing thank you letters to our supporters and killing and preparing chickens for laoka (the side dish eaten with rice) for the Downline mission team coming in a few days to sit down and spend time with You!

As I had many times before, I found the words of Oswald Chambers' daily devotion to be instructive:

> It is easier to serve or work for God without a vision and without a call, because then you are not bothered by what He requires. Common sense, covered with a layer of Christian emotion, becomes your guide. You may be more prosperous and successful from the world's perspective, and will have more leisure time, if you never acknowledge the call of God. But once you receive a commission from Jesus Christ, the memory of what God asks of you will always be there to prod you on to do His will. You will no longer be able to work for Him on the basis of common sense.
> Our ordinary and reasonable service to God may actually compete against our total surrender to Him. Our reasonable work is based on the following argu-

---

[39] Early March 2008.

ment which we say to ourselves, 'Remember how useful you are here, and think how much value you would be in that particular type of work.' That attitude chooses our own judgment, instead of Jesus Christ, to be our guide as to where we should go and where we should be used the most. Never consider whether or not you are of use—but always consider that 'you are not your own.' (1 Cor. 6:19). You are His."[40]

I realized that perhaps I was guided by "common sense covered with a layer of Christian emotion" and was holding myself back from "total surrender to Him" as I lived among the people of Southern Madagascar. No doubt Satan would like to camouflage himself and cause me to be blinded to the true will of God. I guess the enemy tries to deceive us in ways we are not even sure of, since this tactic would cause the Christian to doubt. Certainly Christ's followers might have been more prosperous and successful and have more leisure time if we did not give up our whole lives to follow him. *But the call of God goes beyond common sense.* There was no more denying or brushing over his personal call on my life.

Later that same week, I reflected on the Gospel lesson for the morning, Matthew 16: 24-28: "Jesus said to his followers, if any one of you want to be my follower, you must put aside

---

[40] Chambers, *My Utmost for His Highest*, March 4.

your selfish ambition, shoulder your cross, and follow me. If you try to keep your life for yourself, you will lose it. But if you give up your life for me, you will find it."

This is the truth. When we give our lives to Christ, once and for all, never asking for it back, we gain our life and peace, and joy fills our soul. God will fulfill his promises, and this promise is one of the greatest. His word is true.

Finally, after so many years of fighting the Lord and pulling the rope like a tug-of-war, God won. I was at the end of my selfish rope and had nothing left to pull. I had been relying on myself rather than focusing on his will, acknowledging, "I am his."

Moments of Hope

The Lord was moving among the people of Ankilifaly. The Downline Ministries mission team, led by Kennon Vaughn[41] from the States, confirmed this exciting spiritual growth. Downline Ministries teaches a training program in Memphis, Tennessee, focusing on discipleship and handing the gospel down-the-line by relational evangelism, basically sharing your life with others through discipleship. The Downline group

---

[41] Arrived in March, 2008.

came to Toliara, giving instruction and a five-day training for clergy, evangelists, and selected parishioners from each church. We had met Kennon in our Gordon-Conwell doctoral program the previous year and immediately upon introduction, he exclaimed, "I am coming to Madagascar." Not even a year later, he was at our doorstep.

After a lovely greeting at the airport by a bus full of Malagasy Christians singing their hearts away in joyous welcome to our visitors, the team had pizza, a swim in the pool, and hit the sack at 6:00 p.m. attempting to recover from their arduous journey to get here.

One team member recalls:

> When we arrived in Toliara we received a refreshingly sincere and gracious welcome! About twenty-five members of Todd and Patsy's church waited in the ridiculous heat as our flight was two hours behind schedule (not bad for a 27 hour trip.) When we walked out of the airport, the entire group burst into a song I will never forget. Singing in English at the top of their lungs.... 'You are welcome here, you are welcome here.' The people were filled with life, worship, and gratitude, which gave me incredible sense of joy. Their pride and confidence were contagious, not just in who they were as Malagasy, but as followers of Christ. This in turn gave me a sense of pride and confidence as I considered the far-reaching and soul-penetrating message of the gospel of Jesus Christ and the beautiful diversity of His disciples.

Observing the people in their worship and their attentiveness to the training stirred my spirit. There was such hunger and faithfulness in so many we observed; a desire to hear the Word of Truth that would further their relationship with Christ and enhance their effectiveness in teaching others with the message that had gripped their hearts and saved them. Everything I observed from the people, to the impoverished living condition, to the devoted hearts, demolished and rebuilt my own perspective; stronger, more eternal, more spiritual, less material, more gracious, more compassionate, more worshipful.

The leaders happily spend themselves for the benefit of others in a land that has become their home, loving and living among a people that, from an American perspective, have little to celebrate, but from an eternal perspective have treasure beyond measure and gigantic faith. I can't wait to go back and see them all again![42]

Revival!

Revival was witnessed in what might seem like small ways. There is an elderly man who lives in the bamboo hut next door and sleeps on a grass mat. At night he sees by the light of a single candle. After living here for several months I had only received acknowledgment from him a few times. He sat in his bamboo hut on an aluminum metal chair without a cushion, and waved. Each time he acknowledged me my heart skipped a

---

[42] Shad Berry, July 22, 2011.

beat. Then for the first time, hesitantly sliding one foot in front of the other, he came to church.

Over time, spiritual growth continued to deepen. Almost two hundred and fifty people came to see the Jesus film and learn more about having a relationship with Christ. I recalled the movement of the Holy Spirit through a journal entry.

It's amazing to be in the midst of revival and explosion...heat and energy bubbling from inside causing our hearts to burn for Jesus and hunger and thirst after Him. For the past three days we have been teaching on the Holy Spirit, giving the 20 participants good, solid Biblical foundation and then moving into the gifts of the Holy Spirit. I can truly say I believe God is moving in such a way that this place is on fire for Him—a Pentecostal revival and a power from on high that people are coming to know Him as Savior and Lord and the Powerful One from On High. God is working, things are happening, revival is beginning. People are asking for prayer—they are seeking God more and more. They want to grow in the love and knowledge of the Lord Jesus Christ.

My pen is not even able to move and tell about the greatness of God. It is a mystical empowering of the Holy Spirit. I can only say I believe I am in the midst of such a supernatural work and we serve an awesome God. Praise Him. Amen. Amen. And Amen.[43]

---

[43] March 24, 2008.

Patsy's parents visiting Patsy Fall 2010.
The Gathering Place and well under construction

"Lay Down Your Knife"

Genesis 22 documents God's testing of Abraham's faith and obedience by requiring that Abraham sacrifice his only son, Isaac, whom he dearly loved. Abraham must have doubted, but he got up early and obeyed. Despite his doubt, Abraham trusted. He had three days to turn back, but instead of talking himself out of doing what he believed God was telling him to do, Abraham chose to obey. He called it worship and cut his own wood and built a fire. His son Isaac carried the wood on his shoulders for his own sacrifice, much like Jesus carried his own cross. Isaac wondered, "Where was the sacrifice? Where is the lamb?"

God tested Abraham's faith and obedience, and Abraham was faithful to the end—faithful to the point of lifting his knife. It was only at that point, the point of true obedience, that the Lord said, "Lay down the knife."[44] God takes us to that point, and we must be obedient to the end. The result? All the nations were blessed because of Abraham's obedience.[45]

Obedience precedes understanding. Real truth, at times, is an action of blind faith, incorporated through obedience first and sight second. God doesn't have a Plan B. After five months in Toliara, I sensed the Lord took me to this point of obedient sacrifice. God had seen my sacrifice, my faith, and my obedience. I could be obedient and go to Toliara, deciding again and again to live with the people of Toliara and again and again to return to Toliara—not because of *who* I am but because of *whose* I am. I could never do any of what I do except but for the grace of God. I experienced God putting his hand upon my hand and saying to me, "Lay down the knife."[46] He had seen my faith and obedience, and God was pleased with me. Laying down the knife did not mean I was leaving Ankilifaly. What it

---

[44] Genesis 22:12 (New Living Translation).

[45] Genesis 22:18.

[46] In March, 2008.

meant was that God was showing me the joy of ministry. What was once only a painful sacrifice became the way I experienced the love of God. He was taking my sacrifice and transforming it into a gift from him.

The result? I was able to rejoice and sing, Alleluia!

TESTED
(Genesis 22)

God tested Abraham's faith and obedience
through the sacrifice of his only son,
whom he dearly loved.

He did not know where he was going
and must have doubted,
because God repeated himself, saying, 'Yes, Isaac.'

In spite of Abraham's wonder,
he got up early and obeyed.
In spite of himself and his doubt,
Abraham trusted.

That is faith.

Abraham had three days to turn back;
a three day walk to talk himself out of it.

But he chose to go ahead
with what he believed God was telling him to do,
And called it worship.

Abraham cut his own wood, built his own fire.
His son carried the wood on his shoulders for his own
sacrifice, much like Jesus carried his own cross.

Isaac must have been mystified.
Where's the sacrifice?
We have the wood and the fire, but where is the lamb?

We are the sacrifice.
He is the Lamb.
Rejoice and sing. Alleluia!

My journal entries portrayed a newfound joy:

I am doing my passion. God has created me to
teach God's Word. It started with a degree in teaching
Physical Education so my teaching gifts would be cre-
ative, interesting and interactive—the church can tend
to be a boring contrast to the celebration of life in our
Lord Jesus. We need to make church practical, exciting
and lively!

Secondly, God has created me to serve the Lord
with gifts of hospitality, giving the body of Christ
opportunities to serve the Lord in a very unique environment. Through this gift of hospitality, God has
given his nurturing, Holy Spirit. All God's people are
called to be disciples, making disciples, making disciples. Through dependence upon the Holy Spirit, we
are called to raise up leaders and equip the saints for
the work of the ministry.

Finally, I am called to proclaim this message to
the modern church. As I prepared for two upcoming
workshops; the first on the Holy Spirit for the group

of student evangelists in Toliara and the second for the Episcopal Church Women's Diocesan Convention of Southeast Florida, I realized God was causing me to help bridge the gap between cultures. I was learning to live into my calling, for I have been called by God.[47]

Living among Them

Looking back on those first weeks and months in Ankilifaly, things that had made no sense at the time became vividly clear. Had I not lived in "the box" I would not have understood God's complete calling on my life. If I had not lived in an apartment with no refrigerator, I would not have gotten to see and greet the people downstairs several times a day. If I did not have a front row seat, watching the political coup from my window, I would not have made friends with the *shaman* next door who protected us. If I had not seen Dada Be every day, he would not have trusted me to pray with him. If I had been able to celebrate my favorite American holidays, I would not have learned to love the new holidays of the people I was serving.

As I lived among them, we were learning to trust each other. More importantly, we were learning to trust God. I

---

[47] Ephesians 4:1.

still had much to learn about how to live among these people. Thankfully I did not need to go far to find good teachers. To serve God in Ankilifaly, I began to learn from the Malagasy.

WHERE A YOUNG MALAGASY WOMAN IS FROM

She's from valuing family, community,
relationships, sharing one another's burdens, and prayer.
She lives the day, not guaranteed there will be a next,
wrapped in a cycle of
taking a few coins to the market, buying her daily rice, and
coming home to cook it outside over three stones and
kindling.
She's from a life without privacy and personal belongings.
Everything is another's, all is shared, and material
possessions are held lightly
because in a heartbeat they could become someone else's,
taken away.
She's from living with the belief that she has no choice and
no voice.
She's from thatch huts, tin shacks, and pit latrines,
bathing from the community bucket carried from the local
pump,
using leftover water to hand-wash her family's second-hand
clothes.
She's from living in drought, thirst, and hunger if there is
no water
because she has no means of moving to another town.
She's from life without a toothbrush or shampoo; without a
bicycle, scooter or car;
no health care, little hygiene, and only a primary school
education.
She's from a family of seventeen people
who sleep on dirt floors, crowded beds, and straw mats,
waking to sounds of children playing with plastic bags
and tin cans crafted into soccer balls and hand-made toys.

She's from living only a few feet away from a hut where her
neighbors gather
to pray and sing to the devil, offering sacrifices and libations
to another world.
She's from African Traditional Religion, parents chanting
and evoking ancestors
with haunting songs, playing hand-carved instruments
with goat strings and gourds with seeds.
She's from no to-do list or even a pen and paper to write it,
no goals for the future ~
not a book to read, a table to eat on, lipstick, nor even
shoes.
She's from crowded spaces, dirty places, and through it all ~
Smiling Faces.

Opportunities for Reflection:

Relational evangelism and personal association is more than going to church once a week or even participating in a small group Bible study. It is constantly being engaged in the lives of people.

While living in Ankilifaly, I was stirred by a dream portraying a person with a pitchfork, picking up repulsive trash, piece by piece. Nobody really likes to clean up a trash dump. However, this is when results are most readily seen. The dream encouraged me to persevere in my own circumstances of living with those that God had called me to serve, the poorest of the poor in Madagascar.

As Christians, we need to learn to extend ourselves and go beyond our level of comfort in the world, where another's salvation is purchased by another's sacrifice. After all, this is taking up the cross of Christ.

Reflect upon the following two scripture verses. How do you apply them to your own personal life? Spend time journaling your reflections. Which other scripture verses do you find that apply the same message? How is God speaking to you to utilize these scriptures in your life today?

1 Thessalonians 1:5 (LNT),"And you know that the way we lived among you was further proof of the truth of our message."

1 Peter 2:12 (LNT), "Be careful how you live among your unbelieving neighbors...they will see your honorable behavior, and they will believe and give honor to God."

TAMANA

PART THREE:
LEARN FROM THEM

"Will you persevere in resisting evil, and, whenever you fall into sin,

repent, and return to the Lord?"

"I will, with God's help."[48]

THE BEDROOM WINDOW

"*E*verything has its beauty, but not everyone sees it."[49]

Love is what allows us to see the beauty in others.

As I began to see the beauty of others and love the Malagasy

people, I realized they could truly teach me. I could learn from

---

[48] *The Book of Common Prayer*, 304.

[49] Attributed to Confucius.

them. In Africa, life revolves around relationships. Living in community is something that comes naturally to the Malagasy people. Through living in Ankilifaly and learning from my surrounding neighbors, I began to discern the blessings of laying down my life for another. Beauty no longer came from the natural physical environment of green grass, large trees or a garden filled with flowers. Rather, beauty began to flow from the smiles of the people and from the gentle voices serenading by the bedroom window at nightfall. It was no longer about what I was teaching the Malagasy, but what they were teaching me. Our human minds are unable to learn important information from someone until there is trust in the relationship. By living among them, I was learning to trust them. And they were learning to trust me.

At that time, I was spending many hours a week studying and writing my doctoral thesis. I had it in mind to learn. I chose my bedroom, the most comfortable, coolest place in the house. As I read and researched for my doctoral degree on the bed next to the window, I watched the culture around me. What happened during that learning season was unexpected. The main things I learned did not come from a research article or a book. The priest earning her Doctorate of Ministry would be taught by the Malagasy woman next door.

A few stories illustrate the things I was learning.

Malagasy woman with her prayer book

She's Saving for a Prayer Book

It wasn't a Mercedes or even a two-wheeled bicycle. She was saving for a prayer book. Having just been given a Bible, her smile spread from ear to ear. "Now," she said in Malagasy, "all I need to save for is a *Book of Common Prayer*."

Its equivalency in U.S. dollars would be a cup of gourmet coffee—a *grande latte* at a specialty shop. For her, it was a week's wages, that is, if she had a job. In the meantime, she hoped to gather and sell a few used discarded plastic water bottles and save for a *Book of Common Prayer*. I don't know how she did it. Perhaps she was able to wash some family's clothing to bring in a few earnings. A while later, I saw her turning the crisp pages in her prized new *Book of Common Prayer*. I had been shown through her sacrifice and persiverance the precious value of prayer.

By the Light of a Single Candle

Again, the lights were out. But in spite of the darkness, the faithful believers gathered at the Lord's house during Holy Week to pray through the Stations of the Cross. Ten simply framed pictures, purchased at the local Catholic bookstore, hung by nails pounded into the church's cement walls. As was customary during the Lenten season, the Anglican believers gathered on Friday night, processing from station to station, chanting the sufferings of Jesus.

There was something extraordinary about saying the liturgy by candlelight. Several congregants gathered to read a small book by the light of a single candle, dripping on a woman's calloused fingers. She didn't give a second thought to the melted wax. She was probably used to pain from the burning charcoal embers used to cook her family's rice. Hungry Christians... devoted...searching...seeking...summoned revival in the midst. I had been taught the beauty of the gathered community.

Three Simple Chords

One mid-February day, I went to the women's ecumenical gathering to say "Happy New Year." It was supposed to take place the first week of January, but due to all the political turmoil, meetings had been postponed for a month. I went with four other churchwomen. As is the Malagasy custom, all the churches exchange a gift by presenting a song to the other members of the group. Our quintet was still quite small compared to the other groups. We sang a simple song with three simple guitar chords, coupled with one simple word, "Alleluia."

But it was enough. The people clapped, hooted, hollered! They raised their hands, grinning from ear to ear from the beginning until the end. And if that wasn't enough, the woman giving announcements toward the end of our meeting, gave special thanks to our small group of five, announcing the arrival of a new women's orchestra to Toliara!

All that with a G, C, and D chord. What could be simpler? But when it comes to God, he will take the few tablespoons of flour left in the jar and make a whole loaf of bread. He will take two copper coins and multiply them into thousands. It fulfills the joy in God's own soul when we give him what is already his and trust in him. Because it's not about us. It's all about him. I had been taught who worship is truly about.

COMMUNITY

Today is a beautiful day.
Not because of the weather,
Not because of the size of the house,
Not because I am with all the members of my family,
But because the community begins the day in prayer.
People are practicing the disciplines and that gives them
Beautiful hearts which makes beautiful people
Which makes this day a beautiful day.

Lessons at a Dedication

Everywhere I went, God had new lessons to teach me. This time it was at another church dedication, the Chapel of

St. Andrew in Mahabo.[50] The name on the sign outside the church was spelled incorrectly, but what does it really matter? They got it right inside, and that's the bottom line. It's what's on the inside that counts. With the church's leadership of a young evangelist who loved the Lord and desired to serve God with all his heart, soul, and mind, it was already very active.

The church building was constructed well. Although funds did not allow purchase of pews at first, rented plastic chairs were available for the dedication, and parishioners were assured that the Lord would soon bring the needed money for benches and prayer books. Artificial flowers surrounding the altar and lectionary hinted that the unofficial altar guild had been at work. Dedicated women hand-embroidered a banner saying E.E.M. (Eklesia Episkopaly Malagasy) MAHABO, The Chapel of St. Andrew. A Fanta bottle carried water to be blessed for use at communion, and a former powdered milk container showed practicality for carrying communion wafers long distances undamaged. An uncovered wooden table served as the altar with two single candles in two wooden holders. The linens were to be blessed first by the bishop, and then the newly sanctified altar cloth could be used.

---

[50] November 8, 2008.

The work in Southern Madagascar is hard because there are so many basic needs. Sickness rampages through the congregation with diseases such as typhoid fever and malaria. Gum diseases and open sores ooze and catch flies. One man at the training had not eaten for over a week due to a terrible mouth infection. The body of Christ offered him prayers of healing and celebrated, thanking God, when he finally was able to eat. It's heart-breaking not to be able to give the needed money to all the sick for medical fees, prescriptions, and hospitalization. The average life span in Madagascar is only fifty-six, and in this part of the country it is even lower. "Pity weeps and turns away. Compassion weeps and extends a helping hand."[51] I wanted to learn deeper compassion.

I am comforted by Jesus' words, "The poor will always be among you." He understood the overwhelming anguish of ministering to the poor. Like a flaming fire out of control, Jesus knew their needs could never be extinguished. His reminder is to give the gospel, granting salvation and eternal life no matter how long they live. But does that excuse the fact that we still have to try?

---

[51] Attributed to St. Francis of Assissi.

Twenty-Five Dollars Brings Life to a Soul

One aspect of my ministry in Toliara was to be a "disci-pler" i.e., a person who teaches and mentors others who have become followers of Christ. One week I spent a lot of time at the doctor's in the government hospital checking out the health of one of the girls I disciple from the neighborhood. Since she had never been to a doctor before, she needed a hand-holder to endure the shots and blood tests. The diagnosis came back: syphilis. This was a potentially deadly disease, con-tracted from her mother during birth. After receiving her diag-nosis and buying the first two weeks of prescribed medicines (that's all they had in the store), we came back to the house. Sitting on the bed in the guestroom, the young girl shed tears of gratitude. It is amazing that only twenty-five dollars can save a life and bring hope to a soul.

Unfortunately, we continued to go back to the pharmacy several times to unsuccessfully purchase the rest of the medi-cations needed for full treatment. After eleven months of trekking back to various pharmacies, they were still unable to be found. Desperate, I gathered to pray with the three girls I was discipling. A few weeks later I suggested to the young girl that she and I must walk together again to the doctor and ask him what he would recommend because follow-up treatment with the prescribed medicines was impossible. The doctor requested another blood test. Walking hand in hand to the lab, the young girl took another blood test and the results came back. Negative. No syphilis. The Great Physician had heard our prayer and healed the young girl. Again, she cried tears of gratitude to the loving Heavenly Father who heard the cries of the daughter he had created.

Openness is "the ability to welcome people into your presence and make them feel safe."[52] Again, I was learning from the Malagasy people. Openness was not only an unlocked door into my home; it was an unlocked door into my heart.

---

[52] Duane Elmer, *Cross-Cultural Servanthood* (Downers Grove: InterVarsity, 2006), 39.

Malagasy hospitality – welcoming visitors to their church

Hospitality

The Malagasy are gifted with hospitality. The word *hospitality* comes from the root *hospital*, derived from two Greek words meaning "loving the stranger."

It evolved to mean "house for strangers" and later came to be known as a place of healing. Eventually, *hospitality* meant connecting with strangers in such a way that healing took place. Therefore, when we show openness toward people who are different from us, welcome them into our presence and make them feel safe, the relationship becomes a place of healing. As we welcome people just as they are and invite them to join us just as we are, it becomes a sacred event reflecting what Jesus did for us—providing us with a healing relationship.[53]

---

[53] Elmer, *Cross-Cultural Servanthood*, 43.

The Malagasy truly know how to "love the stranger." Healing was taking place in the slum of Ankilifaly.

Malagasy hospitality – church women
visiting a shut-in in the neighborhood

Learning Noble Character

Noble character. That is what the Lord wants to build in his people.

The irons of sorrow and loss, the burdens carried as a youth, and the soul's struggle against sin all contribute to developing an iron tenacity and strength of purpose, as well as endurance and fortitude. And these traits make up the indispensable foundation and framework of noble character.[54]

Noble character. Years ago in a Christian bookstore I bought a plaque defining the meaning of Patricia. It read, "Noble One." God is still building that in me through my years of missionary service. Praise be to God for the years of suffering, for he is creating iron tenacity. Some call it a strong will or hard head. It can be a strength or a weakness. Either way, it's all to the glory of God.

Even though it is not comfortable, we need to learn to

...never run from suffering, but bear it silently, patiently, and submissively, with the assurance that it is God's way of instilling iron into your spiritual life. The world is looking for iron leaders, iron armies, iron tendons and muscles of steel. *But God is looking for iron saints* and since there is no way to impart iron into His people's moral nature except by letting them suffer, He allows them to suffer.[55]

Maybe this is why many Malagasy are of noble character. Unable to run from suffering, day after day, they bear it silently. How does God restore our soul in the middle of the desert? Perhaps one way is through community. An African proverb depicts this well: "A load shared is half the weight." Living

---

[54] L.B. Cowman, *Streams in the Desert*, ed. James Reimann (Grand Rapids: Zondervan, 1996), 476.

[55] Cowman, *Streams in the Desert*, 476.

with others in community provides encouragement even when life is difficult. Knowing others have survived challenging circumstances helps us, too.

Confirmation

Being a bishop's wife, I sit through and participate in many baptisms and confirmations. Since a short baptismal/confirmation service in Toliara is usually three and one-half hours, I learned to take my journal and document the grassroots happenings of the church. On one such occasion I wrote:

Eight people are confirmed in Anketrika, a big day for them and we thank God for this commitment in their lives. 15-20 people from Ankilifaly have walked 45 minutes in the blazing sun to support the new believers and join this occasion. It looks like a bucket of water has been poured over Victor's head (Victor Osoro, a Church Army missionary to Madagascar from Kenya); he is filled with sweat from head to toe. Yet, in all this heat a young boy just walked in wearing a pair of snow pants. I guess he has a limited wardrobe.

I am sitting next to a woman nursing a very small baby who I guessed to be a newborn, perhaps at most, six weeks old. I have just learned she is seven months old. I wonder how long she will survive.

The Bishop in procession seems to be more like an old man walking with a cane; he has to stoop forward because his miter hits the top of the straw roof of the bamboo church. On Christmas Day when we had communion, Todd removed a fly out of the wine in the communion cup with a wafer before blessing it and had to move the plastic, inflatable Santa Clause hanging from the 5'8" ceiling as it was interfering with his miter.[56]

ONWARD

Worn and ragged, like an old coat,
Moth-eaten and patched,
Used over and over again.
This is the beauty of ministry.
Aching from the journey of self-sacrifice,
Much awaited rain allows me to stop perspiring
And I am refreshed to rest…read…write…pray.

Living Sacrifices

I find myself strengthened, fortified, and encouraged by the letters from God. Uplifted, God's word causes us to smile, even amidst the storm. It allows us to arise when weary and to walk with war-torn blisters. Thank you for fresh perspective on ministry because our spirits are strengthened in God alone.

The book of Romans gives us plenty of wise advice on God's grace, his love, and the battle between flesh and blood.

---

[56] December 28, 2008.

In Romans 12, Paul urges the people in Rome to offer their bodies as living sacrifices, holy and pleasing to God. When we do this, it is a spiritual act of worship.

This chapter of life was particularly trying, considering the political situation in Madagascar. When the Toliara airport closed, and no planes flew back and forth from the capital, I began to wonder what we would do if things worsened. I penned in my journal:

> Todd and I are leaders in the church. Leaders don't flee when times become difficult. Captains don't jump ship. Committed leaders remain with their team until the end. Even if times become difficult, I would say we are called to stay as living sacrifices, counting it as a spiritual act of worship.

OUT MY BEDROOM WINDOW

Out my bedroom window
Pots clang from morning tea,
The shaman's family laughs.
I hear the voice of Fred
The cry of a baby
And the bleat of a sheep.

My mind plays tricks on me
As I desire to interpret these voices.
I block out the challenge of speaking
In a new dialect.
I say it doesn't matter.

I am only fooling myself.
I know it does matter, deeply,
And I wish God would wave his magic wand,
Giving me the gift of interpretation,
Allowing me to better understand
The world around me.

Neighborhood children from Patsy and
Todd's bedroom window

Patsy visits with neighbors

Something in Common

As an MK (missionary kid) Ruth Bell Graham struggled to find her place, her niche, her own sense of beauty. She, too, lived next to a gravesite. From my bedroom window I could almost throw a stone into one of the largest cemeteries in Toliara. Ruth described China as a country of graves. Outside the mission hospital where her father was a doctor, the land was covered by grave mounds and tended by the people who feared the ancestors they worshiped. I was surprised that we had so much in common. "Love them, pray for them, win them, lest they should perish, too."[57]

RUTH BELL GRAHAM

Ruth Bell rode a rickshaw
From the hospital to Shanghai
There is much in common
Between she and I,

Many years have passed
But life is still the same
We are a guest in God's world,
And He knows our name.

She wrote her thoughts,
Journaling at night—with a lamp.
The mission field was her training period,
Her "before Billy" boot camp.

And now I am in training—in Toliara, and its grime
Where the locals live on barely more than a dime,
But for the grace of God, I let my light shine!

Advent: the Season of Preparation

In many cultures, holiday festivities are prepared with presents sheathed in exquisite red ribbon, baked goods with creamy icing, and homes with glittering lights. But do we forget the

---

[57] Graham, *Footprints*, 32.

preparation of the heart? Here in Toliara we are stripped of all the holiday fanfare. Life in the slums doesn't change from day to day. People don't fuss, preparing for Christmas, they are just thankful to be alive.

I was reminded of this when Pierre[58] and I greeted one another one morning.

"Fahasalamana?"

"Matanjaka" (strong) was his answer, grateful because one never knows about tomorrow in the life of an underdeveloped country. Africans never take it for granted that they will arise from their sleep the next morning. Pierre's response was an unknown and friendly admonishment to thank God for the gift of life and lessons learned along the way. Oh there was so much for me to learn!

One Beggar Giving Bread to Another

One day as I walked down the busy street just outside "the box," I noticed an elderly man, dressed in ragged clothing carrying an old plastic bag containing ends of bread given to him

---

[58] Names of all Malagasy characters have been changed.

by the local bakery. Crowded from rickshaws, bicycles, ox-carts and people, the old man and I were squeezed tightly on the sidewalk and came together like droplets of water going down a funnel. Elbows touching, we approached the local beggar, sitting cross-legged in his usual spot, head bowed, eyes hidden under a filthy cap. With his palm extended and raised to the heavens, he depended on a kind passer-by for a mere piece of bread. My sidewalk companion stopped, reached in his crumpled plastic bag and placed a dried piece of leftover bread into the beggar's hand.

This became a clear living picture of evangelism. We are just one beggar telling another beggar where to find bread.

I began asking, what does evangelism look like? I realized, "It is an act of sharing, of refusing to keep something so wonderful and satisfying to ourselves...like recommending a delicious new recipe to friends...if something really matters to you, you won't want to keep it to yourself!"[59] This practical and natural way of sharing faith causes it to be less scary for the new believer. In Madagascar, life-style evangelism occurs on the dirty sidewalk. We are just one beggar telling another beggar where to find bread.

---

[59] Michael Green and Alister McGrath, *How Shall We Reach Them?* (Nashville: Thomas Nelson, 1995), 13.

Almost Too Busy to Pray

In Africa, there is always time for a song and a prayer. In Ankilifaly, the church is right next door to the house of the *shaman*. It is his job to make sure the traditions of the generations are carried on according to the local custom of honoring and respecting their ancestors. Many times the *shaman* works side by side with the local witchdoctor. In the Madagascar highlands, ancestral worship is practiced by family members taking the bones of the deceased out of the tomb, re-wrapping the bodies and carrying them on the family members' shoulders while parading around the village. It is not uncommon to see a cow sacrificed for the ancestors and a portion of the cow's blood poured onto the ground in honor of the ancestors.

As next-door neighbors to the *shaman*, Todd and I had the opportunity to observe the local traditions of African Traditional Religion. In return, the *shaman* also saw Christianity in action. Lifestyle evangelism allows the entire community to observe Christianity in a non-threatening way and a natural environment. On Maundy Thursday of Holy Week, the church has a foot-washing service. But this particular Thursday had been a long day and even priests and bishops' spouses think about skipping church from time to time. Just moments before that evening's Maundy Thursday Service, I considered not going.

Upstairs, busy with my doctoral thesis, I did not want to stop what I was doing. But then I thought about the topic on which I was writing—lifestyle evangelism. I pictured Cindy, Lovely and Masy—the girls I disciple, and I imagined the students I teach, noticing the empty space on the wooden bench where I would sit, wondering where I was and why I was not participating in the foot washing service. What kind of example would I give if I were too busy to pray? Hastily pushing the save button on my computer, I rapidly slipped on flip-flops, descending the stairs into church.

I am glad I did not miss it. As I walked into the church I saw the children sitting together, crossing themselves, bowing in prayer, folding their hands in front of their chest. Children are never too busy to pray. They don't have too many things to do or a doctoral thesis to write. Jesus reminds us to have faith like a child.

I was almost too busy to hear what the Lord wanted to say...

Almost too busy to observe what the Lord wanted me to see...

Almost too busy to listen to the sacred word of God...

Maybe that's one of the enemy's subtle temptations...

Making us think we are too busy to pray...

When all God really wants is our attention.

Madio Ve Ny Tongatrao?

The words of John 13:3-4 began to sink in. "Jesus knew that the Father had given him complete power, he knew that he had come from God and was going to God." So what did he do? "He rose from the table, took off his outer garment, and tied a towel around his waist. Then he poured some water into a basin and began to wash the disciples' feet." My husband, the bishop, led our neighbors in the slum, who had become the church members of Ankilifaly, in performing the same service—washing one another's feet.

Christina, a three-year-old girl from the neighborhood, came to sit on my lap. Dressed in a pink hand-me-down dress, she showed me the silver sequins which spelled "love," in English, on the front of her garment, a stark contrast from her everyday wear of a ragged old skirt with no shirt and no shoes. She poked at the freckles on my white skin and touched the extra connective tissue stretching under my chin and whis-

pered in my ear. "*Madio ve ny tongatrao?*" (Are your feet clean?)
That night as her feet were washed, she must have felt like a
princess. She climbed up on my lap, and it was if God himself
came to give me a hug saying, "Thank you for coming."

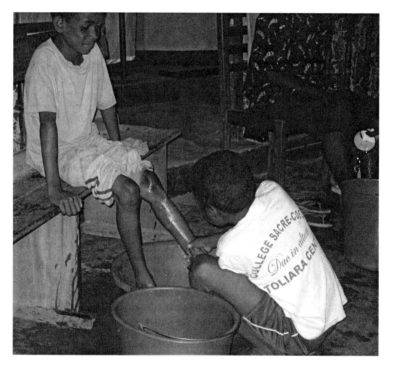

A child washing another's feet at Ankilifaly church

It was a memory in the making. Student evangelists were
washing parishioners' feet; children washing play-mates' feet;
church leaders washing children's feet. Hurriedly I left the ser-

vice to get my camera. Running up the stairs, I noticed the *shaman* tight against the waist high wall with his wife, gazing through the church bricks, watching his family, friends, and neighbors washing one another's feet. The church had become part of the community and now the *shaman* was just inches from the window, observing the blessings of worship and fellowship. Opening the door, I smiled, gave him and his wife a greeting, and ran into the house to get my camera, reflecting, "*This is the church in action.*"

Mivavaka Izy

It was a Sunday afternoon and my heart was filled with joy as I lay on my bed and prayed for all the children who had come to church that day. I rolled over and saw their faces, wide with grins, shirtless and shoeless, waving frantically at the window shouting *Vazaha!* (Foreigner!) A small boy wheeling a rubber tire shook his finger at another, scolding him in a childlike way. "*Tsy vazaha izy, fa Neny Patsy!*" (She is not a foreigner, but Mama Patsy!) I took this as a sign that I had received the Malagasy kids' stamp of approval.

Children showing "Neny Patsy"
a puppy, from bedroom window

I continued my prayer time from the bedroom window and petitioned for many who did not come to church: for the pregnant woman, breasts candidly exposed, cutting her cassava; for the gentleman sitting on a straw mat in the shade next to his bamboo hut; for the young girl cooking beans and rice for her family. I prayed that the Lord would make himself known to the witchdoctor living on the other side of the bathroom window and reveal the truth to those attending the cultist church. As I waved to those walking down the path and gave a kind greeting to the man waiting to talk to the *shaman*, I prayed that the neighborhood would come to know the transformational love of Jesus Christ. With index cards fastened onto the clip board, I dug out a stash of markers and prayed-in-color for the families, asking God to bless and keep them, praying, "Show them how much you love them Lord, and save them according to your promise."[60]

As I rested my head on my pillow and waved to the children outside, I asked God to bless this neighborhood, to send the mighty hosts of heaven to transform this little corner of earth, to reveal the truth and make himself known to this vastly different group of Malagasy people. "Bless the girls I disciple, Lord, as they live here. Cause them to be a strong rock on which you are proclaimed."

Not all the time are we blessed to hear quick, direct answers to prayers. But as I read, rested, prayed and wrote, I heard the words of a small young boy. Pointing at my window, he exclaimed to his friend, "*Neny Patsy. Mivavaka izy!*" (Mama Patsy. She's praying!)

The children. They understand. With their childlike faith they see things which adults don't. I remember one time when

---

[60] From Psalm 119:38-41.

one little girl pointed to the wall of the church and said "*Misy demonia!*" (There is a demon!) She couldn't have been more than three years old and as I looked at the wall, I could see nothing in the earthly realm. But believing that God causes young people to see through eyes of childlike faith, I rebuked the possible evil spirit, taking authority through the blood of Jesus, and told it to get out of the church because we were on Holy Ground.

So Lord…keep us praying…on our knees by the altar in the church, as we prayer-walk the city, and as we embrace the various windows of life. May you send your holy army to redeem our neighborhoods to the glory of God and to the Lamb! Amen!

Celtic Christianity

Realizing that discernment of truth based upon the scriptures is needed when considering all the aspects of Celtic spirituality, particularly with regards to the druids functioning as mediators, I did find the tribal aspect of Celtic spirituality especially interesting in regards to the Malagasy culture of family and their tribal affiliations. Through the relationship with our next-door neighbors and discipleship of a young woman named Lovely, I was able to observe the Malagasy culture first-hand. Like Celtic Christianity, it also has a system in which children of one family may very well be brought up by other family members. It is not uncommon for children to live with aunts, uncles, cousins or even more distant relatives in order to be closer to a school or secure a job. These elders give parental advice and are respected just like the child's birth parent, developing a natural type of mentoring relationship. Because of the traditional belief in ancestral spirits and the "living dead," spiritual oppression is strongly felt in some neighborhoods, as it was in Ankilifaly, but it is never enough to defeat the living God. In fact, it is quite exciting to see the impact that one person can make upon her family.

One day when I was walking down the stairs, I greeted Lovely's grandfather.

"*Salama, Tompoko.*" (Hello, Sir.)

He didn't respond with words but put his hands in a position as if to say he was hurting and in pain. I continued the one-way spoken conversation and inquired,

"*Marary ve ianao?*" (Are you sick?)

He raised his eyebrows the common way as if to say a silent "Yes."

"*Mitady vavaka ve ianao?*" (Are you looking for prayer?)

He raised his eyebrow again to confirm that he wanted prayer for his leg which had been giving him great pain since he had been injured in an ox-cart accident several years ago.

"Ho avy aho." (I will come.)

A few minutes later, Lovely, her elder sister, Victor, two others, and I climbed over the wall, carefully avoiding the latrine and trash pit used by the seventeen extended family members. Approaching Dada Be sitting in his red plastic chair, we noticed Lovely's mother, putting her straw mat under the thatch hut, getting ready for a morning nap. After confirming again with Dada Be that he would like prayer, Lovely's mother continued to stand with us in the group and several other brothers, sisters, friends and neighbors joined us as we laid hands on Dada Be and prayed in English and Malagasy, letting God do his work. A few minutes later we returned to our training and the next time I walked up the stairs, I grinned at Dada Be who was up and walking without pain.

When one looks at this situation with spiritual eyes, several significant aspects can be discerned. First, it was the first time we had ever prayed with Dada Be. Lovely and I had wanted to do this for over two years, but we had waited upon the Holy Spirit for his perfect timing. Sometimes God gives us an idea and we need to wait for particular timing. Secondly, Lovely's mother stayed and prayed with us. She could have very easily walked back into the house but she remained and in addition, several brothers, sisters and neighbors joined us in prayer as well.

A few days before this incident, Bishop Todd and I had invited the *shaman* and his wife into our home for cookies and conversation. Over simple store-bought biscuits and a small glass of orange soda, the *shaman* confessed that he used to attend the satanic worship center next door, just outside our bathroom window. However, he decided to no longer participate in that service and his life was being transformed. In fact, he agreed for his daughter Lovely to continue studies overseas in theology and, during our conversation together, surrendered her to us, giving total spiritual authority to Bishop Todd for his daughter.

Battle Cry

There is a raging war surrounding us; unseen but deadly poison, like carbon monoxide zaps life out of precious souls. As generals on the front line of the spiritual battle, we are taught to pray for daily protection from evil. Deliverance from evil is one of the primary aspects of prayer which the Lord teaches in Matthew 6:9-13.

Many times in my life, I had also allowed the war to go on unseen. However, in Toliara there was no way to ignore the spiritual conflict. Working there taught me to look beyond the mere physical and fight the spiritual battles that truly matter. In Ankilifaly, there was an overhanging oppression. Perhaps it was because of the cultist church outside the bathroom window, on which flew a black flag, a visible sign to the community that they worship the devil. In western culture the evil one disguises himself by working in the lives of people through materialism, perfectionism, moral relativism, and pluralistic faith. In most parts of Africa the spiritual world is not camouflaged. It is as evident as the poverty that slaps us in the face. In Ankilifaly, witchdoctors live within the community, and items used for incantations are sold by relatives of church members just a few stalls from the church gate. Todd and I prayer-walked the city, asking the Holy Spirit to reign his glory upon this place, covering the people of the town in prayer, including rickshaw drivers, prostitutes, children and teachers going to school, the government workers and its leaders. Lord, have mercy upon us.

All are Invited

It would be incorrect, however, if I only saw the spiritual oppression in Ankilifaly. Amidst the battle, I was also learning to have eyes to see the Holy Spirit at work. The Malagasy have grown up in an environment where the spiritual war is evident. They do not hesitate to pray with and for people. They do not just say, "I will be praying for you." Not rushed for time, they stop and pray right then. I was not sure who was teaching whom. As a community of believers, we were learning to do this together, expecting and anticipating answered prayer.

Due to its location in the center of the marketplace of Ankilifaly, St. Luke's Malagasy Episcopal Church had an impact on its neighborhood. Every New Year's Eve the church hosts a praise and worship gala. One year, during the presentation of songs, the sister of one of the girls I disciple stopped in church and sat on a bench. Even though she had been drinking, she felt free enough to come into the church quietly, then to sit and to sing praise songs without disturbing anybody. The following day the girl I disciple came to me and apologized for her sister coming into the church after drinking. Knowing that we had been praying for her sister to come to church for over two years, I smiled at her and said, "*Valim-bavaka.*" (Answer to prayer.) It was apparent that she felt comfortable enough to come into the church and was not alienated by others.

This story shows how I was beginning to have eyes to see God at work in the community. It is also one of many stories of how the church began to meet the needs of the people and bring them into a friendly environment to pray and worship. Just a few months following this event, we saw another.

Blessed to Be a Blessing

God has made us for so much more than we realize. He has blessed us to be a blessing.

Community is the only antidote we have to individualism...we use our gifts for our communities and the body of Christ. We make relationships a priority and share ourselves, our minds, insights, and time with one another. We allow the people in our lives to be who they are and who Christ has created them to be.[61]

It only takes a spark to get a fire going. Perhaps it is one person lighting a match or a piece of coal taken from another's cooking fire. The whole purpose is to help one another get

---

[61] Joan Chittister, *The Rule of Benedict: Insights for the Ages* (New York: Crossroad Publishing, 1992), 44-45.

refined through the combustion, purified by the grace of God, becoming all that God has intended his people to be. When people live in close proximity to each other, they are affected by one another. I was learning and being refined as much as anyone.

Praying-in-Color

One day one of the girls I disciple and I decided at the last minute, to pray-in-color during the noon hour. Specifically we were praying for the future Diocese of Toliara and its church leaders since there was an important meeting taking place in Antananarivo. I was only expecting Lovely and maybe one or two others to come to pray, but within a few minutes about fourteen came, including seven new pray-ers, surprisingly young men in their late teens and early twenties and not regular church attendees. They were just sitting under the tree by the church and when asked if they wanted to join us, decided to come and enthusiastically participated.

The following day was our scheduled day during Lent to pray-in-color during the noon hour, helping to distract the growling stomach during fasting. A few minutes after 12:00 p.m. there were over twenty people in attendance who heard about it from church announcements. Then some older neighborhood children, around twelve years old, wanted to pray-in-color, so I gave them colored pencils and scrap paper and told them not to write on the benches and to remain quiet because we were not just coloring, but we were praying for the future Diocese of Toliara. By the end of the prayer time over thirty-five people were gathered. They brought me their prayer drawings, marked with scripture verses, which I placed in a file for future reference and encouragement, reminding and enabling the church to watch for ways in which our faithful God is answering prayer.

With the church in the middle of the neighborhood and marketplace, people just walking by were able to join in prayer and worship, offering outreach and relational evangelism to those who might be inhibited from entering a formal or secluded church setting. Before becoming a missionary in Madagascar, I would never have acknowledged the importance of something so seemingly trivial as a time to draw and color, but God was showing me the limitation of that thinking. As I was living among the people, God could bring people to do something they wouldn't normally do. Because they saw me on a daily basis they trusted me. My doctoral work, though important, was not more important than these events.

Praying in color

Becoming

The bedroom window became my favorite window. I watched from this window. It was where I went to get centered, where I went to pray, write, listen to music, and look at the stars when the electricity was off, watching hues of the deepening sky. Laying my head on the pillow, I heard faint plucking of guitar strings and humming of a newly created praise song and another original tune. Eyelids drooping, I felt at peace, safe, protected, and loved by my Heavenly Father, finding my place in the world.

The slum had become my neighborhood.

The *shaman* became our friend.

The market seller became a parishioner.

The man who sat on the palm tree became a baptized brother in Christ.

The priest in the window became a student of the Malagasy.

Patsy greets neighbors from dining room window

WHERE I, PATSY, AM FROM

I am from Texas bluebonnet carpets, Indian paintbrushes too.

I am from trying to be at home in seven different states in
twice as many years—
born in the Rockies, learned to read in the Windy City,
learned to drive in Detroit.
I am from a traveling salesman who, when home, read me
books,
and played catch with me in the yard.
Very loyal, he hardly missed a game.
I am from a strong, tennis playing mom,
my high school volleyball, softball, and tennis coach,
who was up for a challenge and eager for adventure.
I am from competition and striving, trophies and
tournaments.
I am from acolytes, altar rails, hard pews, and the *Book of
Common Prayer*,
where faith was private, and I was left to wonder.
I am from an earthly life of country clubs, cocktail parties
and celebration.
I am from traveling between wealth and poverty,
Buckingham Palace and tin shacks, cruise liners and dugout
canoes, soft comfy couches and stones under a tree,
five lane highways and rutty, red clay roads—
the U.S., Madagascar, Kenya, and sojourning back again.
I am from acceptance and rejection,
a web of cultural threads that often catch me by surprise
and shape me and my role in place and time—
at times wearing a clergy collar, at others setting it aside for
a *lamba* (sarong) —
always open to relationship.
In my travels I am always looking for a swim, a shower,
something of beauty,
a quiet place to ponder, a soul-sister to confide in, and the
touch of God's hand.
Now I know, most of all, I am from God.

Opportunities for Reflection:

The bedroom window evolved into a window of prayer and learning, offering intimacy with God. From there I sat on my bed with the window open, observing, pondering, and interacting with the community while writing my doctoral thesis. As the coolest place in the house, it would get a breeze, inviting comfort and relaxation. I could be in that room all day and have peace, putting on music, praying-in-color, and pondering. What in your life offers such peace and intimacy?

How are you learning to listen to God and to those around you? Journal your answers.

Reflect on the statement of St. Francis of Assisi, "Pity weeps and turns away. Compassion weeps and extends a helping hand." How can we, as the body of Christ, express more compassion in this world? In your journal list three ways that you can practically demonstrate compassion in your surrounding neighborhood and implement these into your life-style.

TAMANA

PART FOUR: LOVE THEM

"Will you seek and serve Christ in all persons,
loving your neighbor as yourself?"
"I will, with God's help."[62]

BATHROOM WINDOW

As I progressed in my journey in the neighborhood of
Ankilifaly, I was aware that I needed to learn more
deeply how to love my neighbor. I had faithfully been praying
to grow in compassion, and I knew the Lord wanted to bring
me to the point where my heart would break for the people
around me. Jesus' heart was so compassionate. He wept over

---

[62] *The Book of Common Prayer*, 305.

the city of Jerusalem, and he cried over Lazarus' death, even though he knew he would heal him. This is compassionate care, not just powerful healing. In his great majesty, the Lord took the humble form of a servant and laid down his life for the community around Him.

1 Thessalonians 2:8 speaks to us: "We loved you so much that we gave you not only God's Good News but our own lives too." I needed to learn to love people more deeply, as Mother Theresa exemplified. "The wire is you and me; the current is God. We have the power to let the current pass through us, use us, and produce the light of the world—Jesus."[63] Mother Teresa's call to live among the people and love them is a model for us all. I became intentional in exemplifying her model.

EYE DROPS

Every tear from my eye,
Drops as a seed of compassion
Mourning at yet another transition in this
Life and our place in it.

Moving from one country to another,
One expanded ministry opens another.
Where is home and my place in it?

---

[63] Woodeene Koenig-Bricker, *Listening to God with Mother Teresa* (Huntington: Our Sunday Visitor, 2010), 87.

Tears…seeds of compassion…drop
From my eyes to help me to see
Through the vision of my Lord.

Lord, have mercy on us.

Incarnational Living

"*Incarnation* is the theological word for the truth that the Son of God took human flesh, entered human culture, and lived as we live, but without sin. Similarly, missionaries are called to incarnate Christ in a new culture by understanding and adjusting to local realities and living out God's kingdom values."[64]

Living in Ankilifaly provided many opportunities to live incarnationally. So much was going on, it was like living in Grand Central Station. I recall a time when I was sitting in my cozy study chair. My eldest daughter was checking the oatmeal cookies (oatmeal hand-carried from the States) in the charcoal oven outside, asking if they are the right color brown. At the same time, our second daughter was watching TV while listening to music, and our house helper, Jeanette, was asking me what we needed at the market. Pierre, the guard, also came to the door to ask questions about buying a cooking pot for the

---

[64] Elmer, *Cross-Cultural Servanthood*, 131.

church's five student evangelists who were living downstairs in one single room. During all this activity I remembered my role as missionary and mother. A mother's ministry cannot be separated into systematic departments but must be intertwined with a life-style of love and acts of kindness. Living this incarnational lifestyle of glorifying God and carrying out the Great Commission will have more of an impact on a community than going to a thousand church services.

Life-style (incarnational/relational) evangelism is a natural approach to ministry, beginning with the family and extending to the nonbeliever. Sharing one's faith is the responsibility of all Christians, not solely the responsibility of pastors and church leaders. The word clergy comes from the Greek *cleros* meaning heir or inheritance, referring to *every born again believer.*[65] "Laity" in the Greek is *lao* meaning *all people*, not referring to class or gender. These two above references remind us that every member of the body of Christ is to carry out the Great Commission.

---

[65] Romans 8:17, Acts 20:32.

Making Disciples "As We Go"

Acts 5:28 and Acts 8:4 are prime examples of these principles being lived out as they filled Jerusalem with their teaching…preaching the word wherever they went. One of our professors had reminded us that the Great Commission task is the same today as it was for Christ's first disciples: to live a Great Commission lifestyle and make disciples as we go through our lives.[66] While we are going, we are to do the work of the Lord in whatever context that is. For me in Madagascar, that was while buying chicken.

For the first time in eight months, I went to the only store that sold pre-killed and pre-cut chicken. As I got out of my car, I greeted the man manicuring the lawn, cutting the grass with scissors. I met him once before when he had shown Todd and me small bungalows for guests and a restaurant if we ever needed accommodations to host visitors. When he showed us the rooms, we had a short conversation about two things: his Catholic faith, and rain—why it doesn't seem to fall in Toliara. He said the local witchdoctors pray against it because the locals make their living by making salt and bricks. Rain would spoil

[66] Dr. Robert Coleman, who has written extensively on disciplemaking. *The Master Plan of Evangelism* (Fleming H. Revell Co., 1963)

152

their livelihood. As I turned off the car engine, I remembered his face from before and said "*Salama.*"

He raised his hand as to greet me but could not open his lips to speak. He pointed to his swollen cheek, obviously very painful from an infected tooth. Placing his head in his hands, the pain was so great he almost cried. I walked over to him and spoke.

"*Marary nify ve? Mila mivavaka ve ianao?*" (Do you have a sore tooth? Would you like prayer?)

He looked at me as if to say, "Yes, please," but again, his intense pain would not allow him to open his lips. I laid my hand on his head, prayed a short prayer out loud in inadequate Malagasy, asking God to heal him and take the pain away in Jesus' name. Then I went into the store to buy chicken.

As I left the shop a few minutes later, the man I had just prayed for was deep in conversation with his friend. When he saw me, a huge grin broke out on his face as he shouted and pointed to his cheek.

"*Efa miatsara!*" (It's already getting better!)

I gave him a thumb's up, and pointed to the heavens. "*Misaotra Andriamanitra!*" (Thanks be to God!)

Glory be to God that we can witness and declare his miraculous healing power as we are going wherever the Lord takes us…even to buy chicken. "Prayer is the ultimate love language. It communicates in ways that we can't."[67] Stopping to pray for a few minutes showed this man that I cared. Indeed it did communicate in a way that I could not, especially in the Malagasy language!

Discipleship

Living an incarnational/relational approach to ministry, Todd and I had a great opportunity to naturally share our faith and disciple those in the neighborhood around us. Ultimately a person's own spiritual life is up to him or her. The church is there to assist. 2 Timothy 2:2 reminds the church of the importance of discipleship, mentoring, and teaching one another. The Christians responsibility is to, "…teach these great truths to trustworthy people who are able to pass them on to others."

Discipleship invites others to join in, for example, walking to the market, playing tennis, and going to the beach. It builds a relationship, and that allows praying together often. When someone here had a request, many times we prayer-walked the city. We also prayed for their schooling and education, and over

---

[67] Stormie Omartian, *The Power of a Praying Wife* (Eugene: Harvest, 1997), 29.

time we began to financially sponsor some of the children's education through People Reaching People Inc.

This type of relationship builds trust, and my disciples Lovely, Masy, and Cindy began to confide in me, including me in their everyday activities and asking my advice. This brought me great joy! (My family teases me that I enjoy telling people what to do!) Living in close relationship with others allowed me to live out what I was learning in the doctoral program, providing personal educational and spiritual benefits. Each year we were responsible for reading three thousand pages and writing reflection papers and case studies on outreach, evangelism, and discipleship. This was enhancing my ministry and my spiritual life, solidifying and confirming my purpose in this world, not only to glorify God, but also to bring others to Christ through being a friend. I was learning how to love, in a very different environment than I was used to, with a new dialect of Malagasy and an extremely different standard of living. In spite of the vast deviation, my spiritual gifts of hospitality and nurturing others likened to this kind of outreach, presenting a different type of evangelism than street-corner, crusade, or hut-to-hut evangelism which we generally hear about when discussing evangelism and sharing the gospel.

Revival will be a natural result when Christians realize that private lives and lives of evangelism are not to be separated as oil and vinegar. Evangelism is to be interwoven into a lifestyle of love and caring for others. Hear what our Lord Jesus Christ said: "Love the Lord your God with all your heart, and with all your soul, and with all your mind and with all your strength. And the second is this: Love your neighbor as yourself. There is no commandment greater than these." [68]

Relational Evangelism

March 29 is a Malagasy national holiday, Memorial Day. One year we were visiting one of the more distant parishes in Southern Madagascar, Ft. Dauphin, where the parishioners in Ft. Dauphin were celebrating with a church picnic. We were invited to come early and have lunch at a parishioner's house, and once again the Malagasy graced us with their lovely gift of hospitality. It is a humbling experience to be offered a fine meal consisting of chicken, rice, cucumbers and soda in a home where five people sleep on a double bed, the roof leaks, and they still use an outside latrine and buckets for bathing. But we sometimes honor others most by receiving their kindness and

---

[68] Matthew 22:37-40, (King James Version).

hospitality. This was a time we wanted to honor and learn from them and we saw that their house was a home filled with peace, love, joy, and contentment, just because they were together.

After lunch Todd and I were offered a straw mat, placed outside underneath a tree, a blanket and two pillows for an afternoon nap. Our Malagasy friends took their plastic chairs and joined us under the tree. Their chatter and laughter was a peaceful lullaby, and after a snooze, the men and women took turns playing dominoes. As parents strategized, the children snacked and placed fried corn chips on their fingers as rings, just as I remember doing as a child. Creativity and the desire to play with whatever is available is a worldwide trait.

When it was the women's turn to play dominoes, one woman broke out in song. The words were the Malagasy equivalent to 2 Chronicles 7:14, "If my people who are called by my name will humble themselves and pray and seek my face and turn from their wicked ways, I will hear their prayer and heal their land." It was God's reminder to me that I was doing more than sitting under a tree playing dominoes. I was in the midst of the Holy Spirit's movement in a new land.

As the sun rolled across the afternoon sky, men, women and children left the dominoes and gathered to enjoy a game of soccer. Everyone cheered when their bishop scored a goal by heading the ball through the dead tree stumps representing goal posts on the sandy field. The Malagasy community modeled true fellowship, by just being together and enjoying each other's company. There were no iPods or boom boxes. Just a straw mat, a few plastic chairs, a single wooden table, a borrowed set of dominoes and a not quite fully inflated soccer ball. At the end of the picnic, it was hard to say goodbye... so we didn't. Instead, we said "*Mandra pihaona*," or "See you again." This relational approach to evangelism engages people in fellowship and conversation, allowing people to reach out in hearty fellowship, building trust and a love for one another.

Nothing Boring

One day I was driving with Lovely and Cindy, going to Cindy's house, and I was stopped by the police in town. The policeman said I needed a certain piece of paper attached to my driver's license and since I did not have it, the policeman threatened me, saying I would be punished and taken to headquarters. I was not very happy because I had been stopped by police before and they had never mentioned this piece of paper.

The bottom line was that the policeman was asking for a bribe, as is common for them to do, especially from women. He nonchalantly looked around, waiting for me to place a few bills within the car papers to quietly request that he let me go. This is not the first time this certain policeman had stopped me, trying to squeeze a bribe, but even in the eighteen years of living in Africa I had never paid a bribe, and I wasn't about to start then. So I called Todd to come and provide refuge. As we waited, we saw the policeman stop a few other women, who paid him off, and that increased my righteous anger. After about eight minutes, Todd and the local priest came to my rescue. As they talked to the policeman, Lovely, Cindy and I prayed and bound the evil spirits of corruption, greed and dishonesty, and followed with prayers of blessing for the policeman to be enlightened with the truth. In the midst of my frustration, I was still called to love these police officers. Being with my disciples made it even more apparent that I needed to be a good example, and I couldn't let my anger misrepresent the gospel. Sometimes love requires us to patiently accept, though not condone, an unjust circumstance in order to love our enemy. As I stood up for my convictions, I had to do it in a loving way. We were called to pray for and bless the policemen, not curse them, even though what they were doing was wrong. God was showing me to love not only the just but also the unjust.

Grouchy

If you are like me, there may be a tendency to be grouchy when enduring difficult circumstances. After a short vacation to a national park in Madagascar, I was back in Ankilifaly. It had rained, and since there is no appropriate drainage system in Toliara, the once dusty streets had become a river. Water surrounded us like a moat surrounding a castle, and one had to wade knee-deep in filthy water to cross the street and buy bread. I took a walk in my flip-flops while praying for revival and ended up with a giant blister. As I sat down for breakfast, the chair broke and the electricity was out, once again.

I found relief in keeping quiet and penning my thoughts to the Lord.

> Through all this, I am learning to trust the Lord…to rejoice when the old man next-door waves to me from inside his bamboo hut. His family has strategically placed bricks to use as stepping-stones to his hut because everything around him is underwater.
>
> Every time I come back to the box, it takes a while to adjust—like moving from darkness into light or visa-versa. It just takes getting used to.

I am reminded of the sacrifice through reading Oswald Chambers. "Natural human love expects something in return. But Paul is saying, It doesn't really matter whether you love me or not. I am willing to be completely destitute anyway; willing to be poverty stricken, not just for your sakes, but also that I may be able to get you to God. For you know the grace of our Lord Jesus Christ, that though He was rich, yet for your sakes he became poor. (2 Corinthians 8:9) And Paul's idea of service was the same as our Lord's. He did not care how high the cost was to himself—he would gladly pay it. It was a joyful thing to Paul.

I guess that's the bottom line. I am just way too selfish.[69]

Selfish

My journal entry continued.

It's amazing how selfish one gets when beginning a fast. Yesterday Todd and I started our twenty-four hour Lenten fast—a family tradition during the Lenten season. Since then I've noticed a grouchiness that I can only attest to the selfish desire to feed oneself.

Interesting that when something is taken away, we so naturally crave that which we think should be given to us. Thank God for days of fasting, when we notice our human frailty and then have a supernatural trust in God to overcome our weaknesses. This is not something we do on our own. Only our Lord Jesus Christ can do this for us. Therefore, I became thankful for times of fasting; it helps to refocus, see selfish limitations and modify us into a spirit of prayer, reminding us of the original reason God has

---

[69] February 25, 2010.

created us—not for running water, nor even a hot shower, but to glorify God and enjoy Him forever—while bringing the Lord Jesus to people, living incarnationally with His loved ones down on earth.[70]

1 CORINTHIANS 13
FOR MISSIONARIES

If I speak fluently in the tongues of local languages
and live in a stick and dung hut,
but have not love, I am only a resounding
gong or a clanging cymbal.

If I create the most moving power point presentation,
have a vision for ministry, and have all knowledge
of various ethnic groups, and if I have faith
to build water wells, churches, schools and
health clinics, but have not love, I am nothing.

If I give all my clothing and food to the woman and
child who come to my gate and
walk hundreds of kilometers to preach the gospel,
but have not love, I gain nothing.

Love is patient, it perseveres all culture shock.
Love is kind and forgives when others laugh because
you do things differently.
It does not boast about how much was left behind
or how much was given up.
It is not proud of how God is using you in ministry.
It is not wanting only things bought in western cities,
nor does it delight in easier circumstances.

---

[70] Ibid.

It always protects those created by God.
Always trusts that God is in control.
Always hopes in the everlasting.
Always perseveres when tired or discouraged.
Love never fails.

~~~~~

Bring Your Bible

I received a gentle rebuke from the bishop, my husband, when I chose not to take my Bible to church. It sounds like a relatively easy, black and white issue, why wouldn't you take your Bible to church? But that day it wasn't actually quite that simple.

Church that Sunday was in Anketraka, a brisk forty-minute walk from our home in Ankilifaly. Since we didn't yet have a car, I thought we would take a taxi. But my husband wanted to be an example to the Malagasy people, and live life like they would, so he said we would walk. Having never been there before, I wasn't sure how long it would take, and I had to strategically decide what to carry in my backpack. So, what did I choose? I chose to take out my Bible and journal and instead to carry my tiny Malagasy prayer book, two bottles of water, and a pair of sandals to change into for church. What did Todd carry in his backpack? All the bishop's vestments, the chalice, the communion bread, the wine, the Malagasy prayer book and his thick, heavy, study Bible!

Do you see the difference? I was carrying things for my own personal, physical needs. I had already donned the sunscreen and was wearing a hat and sunglasses, carrying a cloth to wipe the sweat when arriving at church, which Todd used throughout the whole service. I even grumbled along the way because I carried an extra liter and a half of water for the priest who walked along with us. The Lord revealed my selfish attitude and I had much to confess before I took communion that morning!

Todd, on the other hand, had taken supplies to feed the church. Chalice, communion wafers, clergy garb and his *big, very big* study Bible, so he could preach the word of God to the congregation and feed his sheep. Todd was thinking about others and putting their needs before his own. He was living out Christ's love and was teaching me how to do the same.

It's Not Supposed to Be Easy

Dear friends, don't be surprised at the fiery trials you are going through, as if something strange were happening to you. Instead be very glad—because these trials will make you partners with Christ in his suffering, and afterward you will have the wonderful joy of sharing his glory when it is displayed to all the world.[71]

For almost twenty years I had been on the mission field, desiring to fulfill my calling the Lord has given me, but with a major shortcoming: *I had not totally accepted the fact that doing the will of God is never going to be easy, nor is it even supposed to be.* We are called to love, and love is never easy. Peter writes to his readers, "Don't be surprised at the fiery trials." At times, I couldn't even accept the tiny trials and love in small ways, like carrying an extra water bottle.

One school holiday, two of Corbi's friends came to Madagascar for Christmas and New Year's to experience Madagascar during their winter break from Dickinson College. Little did we realize at the time that one of these young men would become her future husband! It was good for him to see our family's life-style, albeit for better or for worse. One day, after driving to several gas stations in town for cooking gas and finding none, wisdom spoke from the young as he saw my frustration and said, "It's not supposed to be easy."

That simple statement helped change my thought process. I no longer had to push and try to make the situation any different. I could relax in the realization that it's not supposed to

---

[71] 1 Peter 4:12-13.

be easy as I was now suffering with Christ and because of that suffering will also share in his future glory (Romans 8:17).

The mind of self-satisfaction shouts, "Comfort! Ease! Instant gratification!" The Christian life reminds us, suffer for Christ's sake as partners in the gospel and during the fiery trials, rejoice and be glad! What a contrast. What a challenge. What a victory when finally done!

Trust

Love requires trust, and trust takes time. Time was one thing we had. There weren't too many other things to do in Toliara. In definition, "Trust is the ability to build confidence in a relationship so that both parties believe the other will not intentionally hurt them but will act in their best interest."[72]

Trust reminds me of the time that Masy, one of my disciples, was finally able to float in the water. I had implored her to come into the water several times before, so I could teach her not to be afraid to put her head in the water, but she was only willing to come ankle-deep. What caused this time to be different? I don't think I will ever know, but when she finally allowed me to hold her body on top of the water, I knew she

---

[72] Elmer, *Cross Cultural Servanthood*, 77.

finally surrendered and trusted me. "Only when people trust us will they listen to what we have to say."[73]

Trust comes in small steps. Only through a variety of experiences is a confident relationship developed. I became thankful that we lived in Ankilifaly, right next to the girls I discipled, so that I could have a variety of experiences with them. I realized that there was no task more important than building the trust of the Malagasy people. Living smack dab in the middle of the neighborhood made the opportunity of learning to love my neighbor possible on a daily basis. God had put me in a place where I could grow in a community of trust and love.

The Bathroom Window

When I first saw the bathroom I was relieved. It had a toilet, sink, and shower. Todd had just renovated this room and it was one of the nicest rooms in the house. The east window revealed gold and orange hues from the sun's rising every morning over the swaying palm trees. The best vista to watch the sunrise was from the bathroom.

However, once the sun rose, the signs of extreme poverty assaulted the eye—garbage, corrugated tin wedged on bamboo

---

[73] Marvin K. Mayers quoted in Elmer, *Cross-Cultural Servanthood*, 76.

huts, the ever-present small white plastic bags that lay wherever they landed until the next breeze carried them to another twig or log on which to rest. And the signs of extreme poverty also assaulted the nose when one looked down, directly below the open window. A neighbor's latrine was below, and looking out I could not escape the flies or the stench. A constant, unpleasant malodor wafted in the breeze.

Neighbor's latrine and garbage
directly below the bathroom window

And then there was the black flag whipping in the wind on top of the tin roof that rested on the top of a small but very bright yellow building. The flag represented the devil-worshiping church. It was alarming to wake up at 5:30 in the morning to the sounds of someone worshiping Satan. The bathroom represented a dichotomy of the beauty of God's creation and the uttermost ugliness of evil and poverty. There is something perplexing about going into a bathroom to clean and purify oneself, while realizing that one's neighbors are engaged in truly oppressive activities just outside the window. I could feel the oppression, and at times in the early morning hours before the 6:00 a.m. community devotions in the one-room church next door, I would go outside and spiritually sweep the surroundings, cleansing the evil spirits and claiming God's holy ground.

Cultist church, on which flew a black flag,
from Patsy and Todd's bathroom window at sunrise

169

One day a girl began manifesting evil spirits and her family forced her to go to the building with the black flag. They would put charms and witchcraft medicines on her skin. The evil was so present and the Christian light was becoming so bright that the evil forces were being threatened. Later, we brought the girl to our church, where we tried to deliver her from the evil spirits. They spoke and said that there were seven. We felt she was delivered from four but three still remained. My heart poured out in prayer for the people surrounded by such adversity and evil. I prayed that they would grow in the grace and knowledge of the Lord Jesus Christ and that God would grant them grace to live a life of love, through the Spirit who now dwells in them. Later that night I wrote in my journal:

> This morning I woke up to pray for the next-door neighbors living behind our bathroom window. I can see a bit of hesitation, a bit of doubt in their eyes. I sense they are a bit uncomfortable with all of this -- the tension between the revelation of Christ in their midst and the evil practices that continue only within eyesight of the church. Lord, please fill their hearts. Cause the seed that has been planted to grow to bear great fruit. Cause eyes to open, the scales to fall from their eyes and enable people to trust you. Lord, have mercy upon them. You have called them. Cause them to come.

Jesus drove out an evil spirit from a man that could not talk.[74] That story sounded like the experience of another girl in our neighborhood who couldn't seem to speak. But God worked in her heart and she even came to church one Sunday. To my knowledge, it was her first time in three years.

This window had my attention. From here I would observe friends and church members using a pail filled with soapy water to do their washing. Children turning upside down in handstands and revolving in cartwheels would urge others to try to ride an adult bike much too large for them while singing the songs they just learned in Sunday school. I observed an old man sitting on the stump of a palm tree. For two years I prayed for him without ever meeting him or knowing his name. My heart rejoiced on the day I finally shook the gnarled, calloused hand of this impoverished elderly man when he came to church. He was later baptized and carried his Bible as proudly as an American teenager would shine his first car. When he passed away, I watched the women weep at his bedside, and tears rolled down my cheeks. I attended his funeral, wore a *lamba,* and walked to the burial ground with my other friends from the neighborhood.

Last I knew, the flags were still flying at the cultist worship center, but the building was locked up with chain and lock and

---

[74] Luke 11:14-24.

there was no singing to signal a morning alarm. Thankfully, we haven't heard the music for a long time. The Africans have a saying: "God is everywhere." I was certainly glad I knew he was with us in Ankilifaly.

So even among the oppression and evil, the cultist church and the ugliness, God challenged me to fill my life with prayer and love. I was not to give up on my neighbors or this land. Through love, we can make a difference, even when it seems small. God is pleased when we learn to love the people around us.

A VISITING U.S. MISSIONARY'S UNDERSTANDING OF WHERE THE MALAGASY ARE FROM

African reggae harmonizing, babies' tears
and children's squeals.

They say come and drink the sacrament of suffering.
Life together is life.

Chestnut eyes scan charred fields
swallowing dust from which we came.

To come here is to say "Yes."
"Yes" to the hospitality of those who give you their best,
their lemur napkin, and the one piece of meat they could
put in the *loka*.
Widows placing pennies at the feet of Pharisees

To say "Yes" is to accept.
Don't fix, just live.

Be baptized anew
one cold river, twenty-five naked catechumens.

Here, the blood of Christ is Fanta mixed with
Air France Merlot
Bread of life, rice served by the ones you're supposed
to be serving.

Doubts, all those previous "Did God really?"
fall away as I sit at the fragile table, scooting my
breaking chair.

This is my Body, take, eat.

All the humor, those botched *Salamas*
all gifts and gracious smiles
To step into the loving embrace of the other is to
wade into the Waters of Siloam.

The voice whispering, "Where were you when I laid the
foundation of the world?" Whispers "Here I am," as a
nursing mother.

Color caked in dust.
Lambas (sarongs) hiding wisdom wrinkles.
College degrees can't teach that.

Vazaha (a foreigner), yet family.

Opportunities for reflection:

Through my experience in Ankilifaly, I found that beauty no longer depended on superficial beauty of nicely manicured lawns or a garden filled with flowers. I realized that true beauty comes in the depths of watching people come to faith. The man who sat for two years on the palm tree became the symbol of beauty from the bathroom window, representing a transformed life and a brother in the Lord. The beauty was preaching a sermon and feeling his calloused hand in mine as I looked into his eyes after church and said *"Faly mahita anao,"* (Nice to see you here).

What is it in your life that shows you beauty? What are you learning from God about beauty and love? Has God ever called you to love something or someone who, in some way, was not "beautiful" or easy to love? How does God see things? How can God transform what is "ugly" in the eyes of the world, into an object of beauty and love? Record these thoughts in your journal.

1 Thessalonians 2:8 speaks to us. "We loved you so much that we gave you not only God's Good News but our own lives, too." How can the body of Christ learn to love people more deeply, as Mother Teresa exemplified in her life and statement, "The wire is you and me; the current is God. We have the power to let the current pass through us, use us, and produce the light of the world—Jesus."[75] Spend a few moments recording these thoughts in your journal.

---

[75] Attributed to Mother Teresa on numerous web sources.

TAMANA

PART FIVE: START WITH WHAT THEY KNOW

"Will you . . . respect the dignity of every human being?"
"I will, with God's help."[76]

THE KITCHEN WINDOW/PORCH

"I Am Because We Are."[77]

*T*he people of Madagascar have one thing in abundance: community. African theologian John Mbiti proclaims the true state of the African as being in existence because of the

[76] *The Book of Common Prayer*, 305.

[77] John S. Mbiti, *Introduction to African Religion* (Nairobi: East African Educational Publications, 1991), 118.

community around them. The African thought process revolves around community. People exist because of the community, not because of who they are as individuals, but who they are in relation to the community. The Western church can learn from Africans and how they value community. Whenever they have a gathering, everyone is invited. Daily routines are performed in community. People harvest their fields in cooperation with one another, pound rice in synchronization, wash clothing side by side at the river, and gather water at the well, together. Taking part in things individually is a foreign concept and is frowned upon as it devalues others. Applying this thought process to a spiritual level will invigorate the church throughout the world as Christians learn to escape myopic vision and focus on the needs of others, serving one another in love, as Christ loved the church.

Malagasy Culture and Community

Upon arriving at the airport in Antananarivo, passengers receive a pamphlet that contains Malagasy history, traditions, and current events. The July/Aug 2010 edition contained a special article regarding fifty years of culture in Madagascar. One of the three fundamental elements of Malagasy culture described is the concept of *fihavanana*. This is the idea of the close kinship all humans share with one another. We are a community.

The Malagasy people exemplify the true meaning of community. When we learn to respect the dignity of all people, we learn this concept of *fihavanana*. Not in the traditional culture through invoking the ancestral spirits, but in harmonious living in the spirit of brotherhood. People are created in the image of God, and focusing on this fact will instill hope and help eliminate a judgmental spirit, which causes division and ultimately destroys the body of Christ. With this spirit, the person at the gate asking for rice can now be seen as a person to help, not a disturbance. The vanilla seller at the market is no longer a pest but a mother of five gathering hope for her children's education. I had to learn to respect the dignity of all people.

God calls us to see each person as God sees his child. I was being stretched and urged by the Holy Spirit to ask the names and to hear the stories of the beggars at the airport. I met a crippled man named Pascal. I learned he rode his wheelchair for miles every day, just to keep fit and work out his upper body in order to compete in the Malagasy equivalent of the Special Olympics. I began to wave at him when I saw him great distances away from Toliara, in the heat of the day, wheeling his chair up inclines, just to be fit.

I learned that Dame has been blind for life. His sister's eyes became his refuge as she led him from one traveler to the next by placing his hand on her shoulder. Finally, I realized that Gasy, on crutches, is a father of two. As expressed in the baptismal covenant, we are to learn to respect the dignity of all people. Through a kind gift from a priest and his wife visiting while on sabbatical, Gasy was given a wheelchair, and could then wheel himself to church. One day he suddenly passed away while we were out of the country, and the local church members went to his family's house to pay respect. In retrospect, I am truly thankful to have learned from Gasy and believe we will one day see one another again as we praise the Lord together in eternity.

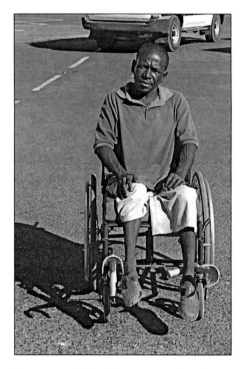

Gasy, one of the beggars at the airport,
wheeled himself to church

Acceptance

"Acceptance is the ability to communicate value, worth,
and esteem to another person."[78] As a guest in the Malagasy
culture, I knew I had a lot to learn from my Malagasy brothers
and sisters. Learning from them moved us into strong and
trusting relationships not enforced by colonialist attitudes and

---

[78] Elmer, *Cross-Cultural Servanthood*, 58.

dependency. The Malagasy began to realize that we did not come to change them, but to live among them with respect and honor, accepting them, promoting unity. "Accepting one another may be among the most powerful acts of love we can offer to each other because it promotes oneness."[79]

"If we do not accept as good, God's shaping of our person and life in our own culture, we will never be able to accept his work in the lives of others who are culturally different from us."[80] We needed to appreciate the good of our own selves and our own culture first. Then we can accept theirs. This will enable enactment of the Great Commandment—to love another as ourselves.

Prayer

In order to do this, we need to live a life of prayer. I was inspired by the words of E.M. Bounds:

> The heart and soul of ministry is in our prayer life. It means the closet first, the study and activities second. It is a most serious work of our most serious years, the char-

---

[79] Elmer, *Cross-Cultural Servanthood*, 60.

[80] Sherwood Lingenfelter and Marvin Mayers quoted in Elmer, *Cross-Cultural Servanthood*, 57.

acter of our praying will determine the character of our preaching.[81]

Prayer freshens the heart of the preacher, keeps it in tune with God and in sympathy with the people, lifts his ministry out of the chilly air of a profession, sanctifies routine and moves every wheel with the facility and power of a divine unction.[82]

Talking to men about God is a great thing, but talking to God for men is greater still.[83]

Pauline Epistles

Someone gave me wise advice during travel—to think of myself as Paul did, spreading the gospel everywhere I went. So I adapted the name to Pauline and on a trip to Ft. Dauphin in the Southeast of Madagascar, my travel log began. On the plane, a woman I had never met, sitting next to me, asked me to pray for her, as her sister just died and she was going to the funeral. She must have had a clue that we were Christians from the big cross around my husband's neck. As we held hands and prayed, I remembered the advice I was given, to be Pauline and carry the gospel wherever I went. I was so thankful that this woman, like most Malagasy people, was very eager to speak with us about spiritual matters and even initiated the conversation. The Malagasy already have a belief in the *Zanahary*, the

---

[81] E.M. Bounds, *Power through Prayer* (Grand Rapids: Zondervan, 1962), 31.

[82] Bounds, *Power through Prayer*, 28.

[83] Bounds, *Power through Prayer*, 31.

omnipresent Supreme Being, omnipotent Creator and regulator of the life of mankind and of the world. Therefore we can start with what they already know, an omnipotent God, and share with them that the omnipotent God loves them and has sent his Son Jesus Christ.

The day after that, when traveling to an out-of-the-way village, the car broke down for the fifth time and we were resigned to walking. On the way, we were greeted by singing Christians who normally walk over ten miles to church. They were ecstatic that this time we came to greet them in their village. In that village there was a child, not yet one year old, suffering from what must have been water on the brain. She had a head the size of a helium balloon and her eyes rolled back, revealing only the white of her eyes. It was heart wrenching. I thought about my eldest daughter and the papers she had been writing for her neuroscience degree, which included a case similar to this very child's. Sadly, there was no one here with any neuroscience degree, or any doctor at all. The Malagasy people did what had been ingrained in them through their cultural belief in a powerful God. The church community prayed for the small girl and asked God to meet the family's needs even when the situation seemed hopeless. They had always believed, even before they were Christians, that there was a powerful God who could help them in their situation. Now as Christians, they knew that God cared and was listening. They knew God personally.

The next day we laid the cornerstone for the first Anglican Church in Ft. Dauphin[84], conducted a baptismal service for about twenty new Christians, and finished morning services at 1:00 p.m. During the service I was amazed to think that whole families were coming to know Christ. Fathers, sons, mothers, daughters, grandparents, aunts, uncles, nieces, and nephews were all baptized together into the family of God. Serving Christ and seeing the Holy Spirit work in people's lives is such a privilege.

Who Is More Content?

Following the service we were invited to the priest's house for rice and chicken with cucumber and carrots marinating in vinegar, allowing just enough time to take off my shoes and lie down on their children's bunk bed for a twenty minute nap before the ecumenical Memorial Day service began at 3:00 p.m. I am glad I was the bishop's wife and that my duties subsided after the second service, as I could come back to the

---

[84] March 27, 2010.

house, rest and shower before dinner. My husband, on the other hand, listened to two more hours of confessions before the next day's confirmation service!

I waited for the bishop and wrote an email to my friends and family:

> As I sit on top of a hill in the dilapidated Lutheran church used for today's confirmation service, I watch the ever-changing orange hues as the sun sets and the cruise ship pulls out of port. God has given the cruise ship travelers from South Africa a lovely day in Madagascar with a cloudless blue sky and weather in the 80s (but in church it was close to 95!) It is ironic to think that I am watching the first cruiser to come to the new port in Ft. Dauphin as I chat with a group of women who make straw mats by hand, using them as beds on which to sleep.
>
> During our conversation, we talked about age, because one woman's husband was confirmed today at the age of eighty-seven. Imagine having your first communion at eighty-seven just because you never before had the opportunity. As we watched the ship fade into the distance, I asked one woman how old she was[85], and she said she didn't know because she never went to school nor learned how to count.
>
> And now I am writing this message on a blackberry to friends and family who will receive it even before the women who attended the meeting will get home, as they walked over an hour to get here.
>
> Sometimes the incongruities overwhelm and life seems out of balance. I can see that Jesus was right when he said

---

[85] This is not a rude or uncommon question, as it would be in other cultures.

blessed are the poor. The boys that play with a soccer ball made of rope and torn plastic bags laugh wholeheartedly when they kick the rock set up as a goal marker. The girls knock ping-pong ball sized rocks on the ground in a game of telling stories of friendship and playing house. Babies smile and coo at their mothers' breasts as we chat and I realize that a fellow Anglican sitting beside me walked seventy-four kilometers last week to a ladies meeting, accompanied by her husband. Why did her husband walk with her forty-four miles to the ladies meeting? He had to guide her. She is blind.

And the people on the cruise ship take showers after their day of seeing lemurs in the endangered rainforest of Madagascar, getting ready for a gourmet dinner and dancing. Perhaps they even try their luck in the casino. Two different worlds pull apart as the cruiser sails out to sea. I ponder and wonder, 'Who is more content?'

I am blessed to have been able to experience both extremes. The ship was far out to sea when the women turned around and gazed, astonished when the priest's wife told them that the Bishop and I had been on a boat like that—three times—for three different cruises!

I call it a privilege to host visitors and mission partners from the western world, allowing them to see the Malagasy side of life as well as explaining other cultures to our co-workers and fellow Anglicans in Madagascar. I understand the words of Jesus more today than I did yesterday. I see contentment in the eyes of the Malagasy people and the Word of God stands true. Blessed are the poor in spirit, for they shall see God.

The Malagasy were seeing God because they knew their need for Him. Not bogged down by the worries and comforts of this world, they have time to enjoy God's presence and to enjoy the presence of one another.

Stark Contrasts

The contrasts found in Madagascar are mind-boggling. An incredibly beautiful island with loads of natural resources[86]—flora and fauna found no other place on earth—exhibits potential, but at the same time a lack of leadership and an abundance of political corruption have led the country into despair. People and other nations want to help, but because of the Malagasy politicians' abuse of funds, they withdraw financial support. The Malagasy people are twisted into a state of fatalism, resignation, and hopelessness, especially in the South. According to United Nations statistics, seventy percent of the people are food-insecure[87], and Madagascar has the highest

---

[86] The world's largest sapphire was found in Madagascar.

[87] Food security refers to a household's or country's ability to provide future physical and economic access to sufficient, safe, and nutritious food

percentage of child malnutrition in the world. If not assisted, this situation will likely erupt into a humanitarian catastrophe.[88]

These contrasts are seen on a daily basis, such as the time we attended a church picnic and were invited for lunch at a parishioner's home. The hostess was employed by the government as a teacher at a primary school, and housing was provided for her and her family. But her family of seven could hardly squeeze into the tiny wooden shack with a tin roof. I could see light through several holes in the roof and buckets lining the floor to catch the frequent rain. The school was located on the edge of a rainforest! The teacher and students use a pit latrine and teach and learn in a dilapidated school building with no textbooks, chalk, or blackboard.

I was not sure what the Lord was saying to me at that point in time. I felt his presence, his closeness. I was also aware that he wants his children to be looking out for something, learning from him, watching and learning from the parables along the road of life. I was a bit weepy, usually signifying the Spirit sensitizing and preparing me to be aware of his presence so I don't miss it. It's a good thing, but I can't always explain it. It

that fulfills the dietary needs and food preferences for living an active and healthy lifestyle. FAO Agricultural and Development Economics Division (June 2006). http://en.wikipedia.org/wiki/Food_security (accessed 18 Dec. 2012).

[88] United Nations report, July 25, 2011.

is another one of God's mysteries. My tears also could have been the result of God's answering prayer for me to grow in compassion and go beyond superficial love, gaining depth of insight from the Malagasy people. Maybe God was preparing me to hear the history of Ft. Dauphin the following day.

Bondage and Slavery

Before we left Ft. Dauphin, we went to the old fort and museum for a historical tour. The history of this port city is interesting as well as challenging to learn about. In short, the area was developed by foreigners for their own selfish desires. According to the story teller who led me around the museum, the second French governor, Flacourt, brought the Malagasy people into an abusive state of slavery for almost two hundred years (1663-1848).[89] The Malagasy people were captured and sent with their families to Reunion Island, a French colony, to work the sugar cane fields and coffee farms. In order to get to the small ship awaiting them in the ocean, the slaves would march through a tunnel, yoked by the neck in a single file line. Chained iron rings welded to their arms and legs needed to be

---

[89] That is one reason why there are so many replicas of slave bracelets sold in the South, but many Malagasy have no idea that they represent the horrors of the past.

severed by chisel if there ever was a chance to be set free. Slave drivers forced helmets on their heads and used pieces of iron to gag and force the slaves' tongues down as they whipped them with chunks of rhinoceros hide. When the slaves finally walked through the tunnel and neared the ocean, they continued to stumble across the slippery coral reef, single file, climbing into a small boat which transferred them to the larger ship to Reunion. When arriving at Reunion, they stayed for forty days and were treated for tropical diseases before they were sold, reminding me of fattening the calf before the slaughter.

I guess what greatly impacts me is the realization that the Malagasy people remain in a state of despair and are still reaping the consequences of the misdeeds of others. Because of others' greed and fulfillment of selfish desires, the country and its people remain in a state of suffering. With a land of overwhelming beauty and potential and such accommodating and welcoming people, this country could be excelling. Yet the cycle of poverty and desperation continues.

This is a great place to start when sharing the gospel with the Malagasy people. They know what it means to have been in bondage and slavery, but no earthly power or government has been able to bring them out of despair. When people do not know Christ they live a life of bondage and oppression. We all need the eternal Savior and Redeemer, Jesus Christ. Thank God for the freedom we have when we know Christ as our Savior and Lord! May God give us the grace to do his work here in Madagascar to his glory and to the benefit of the people and their communities, their churches, and their country.

Fruits of Labor

While Todd was still a priest, several years before we moved to Toliara,[90] he and I came with our daughters to Morondava during the first church plant. Ten years later[91] we saw many fruits of that labor. Over a period of three years, nine new churches were planted in the Morondava parish. During one pastoral visit, Todd baptized eighty-eight people, confirmed fifty-eight and performed one wedding. I also was able to participate, preaching in Malagasy, praying over the children, and assisting with communion. Just as communion was about to be distributed, lightening cracked and thunder roared as nature reminded us of the powerful God who had really been at work

---

[90] In the year 2000.
[91] In January, 2010.

in Morondava. In between those packed services, we taught the women to be faithful in the home, faithful in the church, faithful in evangelism, and faithful in giving respect to their husbands. Several church members walked a round-trip total of thirty-six miles to participate in this event.

During that trip to Morondava, we marathoned two four-hour church services and a tropical depression. We even had to construct a device to wade over the water to get to church. Due to the high tide, the full moon, and rains from the tropical storm, a make-shift bridge had to ford the knee-deep water, allowing us to finally make it into the church building without soaking wet trousers. It took us an hour and a half to go two and a half miles because two different cars broke down three times. At first the owners of the first car thought it was because there wasn't enough gas, so their twenty-year old daughter took a plastic can and walked to the local petrol station. Upon her return, the father folded a piece of cardboard to funnel the gas into the car, but to no avail. The engine was as difficult to turn over as a teenager who wanted to stay in bed. Knowing that it was nearing the time to start the service, we opted to walk to the main road and hail a taxi. However, there were none available, and we waited almost twenty-five minutes to find a mode of transportation besides an ox-cart. Finally, we squeezed into a public *taxi-busse* with standing room only, which broke down twice, the final time—thanks be to God—right in front of the church! The good thing is the bishop is never late because services will not start without him.

Lunch was served between morning and afternoon services, and Todd met with clergy, church leaders and evangelists and squeezed in a three hour interview with Malagasy elders for his doctoral research, while I took a nap. When it came time to leave for church again, I decided to walk. It was not the refreshing walk I expected, but it showed me something about the Malagasy people I will never forget.

Miaraka isika—We Are Together

I knew it would take about an hour to walk to the church, but I needed to get my blood circulating after traveling and sitting in churches. I was escorted to the main road by the daughter of our hosts. After a statement of thanks and quick good-bye, I began the journey along the unpaved road and was soon covered with mud as a result of the tropical depression the night before. Being one of the only white women in a small town can either boost or demolish an ego. This time it was an unrequested "boost," if the stopping of several men to offer me a ride is the measuring tape.

The woman I passed on the road moments before saw what was going on, that it would be dangerous for me to accept a ride from a stranger, and stepped up her pace after she heard the last invitation from a man asking if I would like to hop on his motorbike. The woman came to my aide, boldly proclaiming,

"Miaraka isika." (We are together.)

Seeing my plight, she stayed at my side like an obedient guard dog beside his blind master. We chatted until her destination, the local market where she purchased her rice and daily *loka*. At that point I was surprised to see a student evangelist and a catechist from church who rode their bikes to my side. They were intrigued to see that I was talking and walking with a companion along the road. My new-found friend told the two church leaders the story and they took the reins as substitute guard dogs, escorting me the next twenty minutes to church.

I Am Because We Are

As seen here, some cultures demonstrate a protection for others, keeping an eye on their neighbors. "We are together." Not even knowing my name, this woman took me into her care, depicting love, protection, and the security of being in community. John Mbiti's words rang true. "I am because we are."

I remember that this concept became a point of discussion with those living in the international, married housing units at seminary when we attended Trinity Evangelical Divinity School in Deerfield, Illinois. Several people expressed concern to the resident advisor about the African children playing in the parking lot, thinking that they might get hurt. Condemnation and a judgmental spirit began to divide the community, as parents from one nationality thought parents from another were neglectful. The issue ended up being a cultural issue. The African culture realizes the importance of community and expressed their expectation that the other parents should, according to the African culture, reprimand their African children, since "it takes a village to raise a child." However, scolding another person's children is not an accepted concept to an American, and the American students and family members had no idea what was being expected of them. Misconception and expectations needed to be settled to bring unity back to the community, enabling all to proclaim, "We are together."

I Fall to My Knees and Pray

This cultural difference made me think. Was I agonizing over the Malagasy church, loving it, protecting it and caring for it like this woman, whom I met walking on the road had done for me? Or was I neglectful, thinking it another person's responsibility to keep an eye on the spiritual "parking lot," watching out for the sacred lives of others?

The Apostle Paul agonized over the church in Laodicea, and for many other friends whom he never knew personally.[92] He prayed for spiritual empowering for the people of Ephesus.

> When I think of the wisdom and scope of God's plan, I fall to my knees and pray to the Father, the Creator of everything in heaven and on earth. I pray that from his glorious, unlimited resources he will give you mighty inner strength through his Holy Spirit. And I pray that Christ will be more and more at home in your hearts as you trust in him.[93]

Will we allow the Spirit of God to bring us to do the same?

---

[92] Colossians 2:1

[93] Ephesians 3:14-17 (New Living Translation).

I Am with You and Will Watch over You Wherever You Go

I realized that not only were the Malagasy people thirsty for God, God was thirsty for them and longed for them to be a part of his kingdom—his community. I marveled one night as I read God's word to Jacob: "I am with you and will watch over you wherever you go."[94] God was with Jacob, even at times when Jacob did not realize it. God had been shaping his life and caring for him. I marveled that the same God of Jacob was the God who cared for these Malagasy people. He had been working in their lives and watching over them long before they even realized it.

Over a hundred people squeezed into a temporary wooden structure, quickly constructed to replace the grass hut that previously held church services. It was only the size of an American garage and contained six planks of wood on each side of the aisle for seating. People from miles around had come to be baptized into the church or to confirm their faith in the Lord Jesus Christ. People unable to find space on a bench sat on the newly poured cement floor or looked in from the

---

[94] Genesis 28:15.

windows. Eager to watch, they observed what was happening in their community.

"I am with you and will watch over you wherever you go."[95]

Several people, refreshed and given new life by the Spirit of God, joined the Anglican community: small babies still dependent upon their mothers' nourishment; elderly ladies with salt and peppered charcoal-covered hair; some girls dressed as brides, complete with white dress, veil and gloves; others barefoot, bearing white hand-me-down shirts with holes eaten by night-critters. All were equal in the sight of our Lord.

"I am with you and will watch over you wherever you go."

Thirsty new believers, hungry for the gospel of Christ, gathered together to worship the Lord Jesus, dropping their farm tools in mid-week harvest, desiring to be part of something that was bringing hope to their land. It was a privilege to watch and participate, spreading the gospel of the Lord Jesus Christ.

"I am with you and will watch over you wherever you go."

---

[95] Genesis 28:15, (God's Word Translation).

The Land of Plenty

It brings a hopeful reminder to us when we realize that wherever we are in the world, the Lord watches over us. Frequent travels for our Doctorate of Ministry program at Gordon-Conwell Theological Seminary caused us to flip-flop across the oceans. Extreme situations aroused thoughts regarding both sides of these divergent economic conditions. I was in America, and got a phone call from my husband, relaying the message he received from some church parishioners in Madagascar who had to flee their village because they did not have enough food to eat nor water to cook their food. Locust and drought had robbed them of harvest two years in a row. I was shopping at a grocery store when I got the call.

I was now in "the land of plenty" and along with the abundant choice of delicious food and drink we had the variety of options...walk the beach...go for a jog...watch the sunrise...swim in the pool...read my Bible poolside...write in my journal...read my new Christian book...sit by the inter-coastal canal...rest in the hot-tub...sit on the porch...stay in bed...check email...call a friend. Too many nice things can be quite a distraction. They are like the "no-see-ums" by the canal—hardly visible, but even so, a nuisance and distraction. Are the options we have perhaps the same—distractions from the simplicity and deeper meaning of our lives? Is this an unseen trap and part of the enemy's plan to distract us from what is really important?

I Miss Africa

When I was living in the States, I began to miss the simplicity of Africa. I missed the very small bamboo hut with standing room only that served as a church building. I missed seeing the offering taken in a New York Yankees baseball cap as I worshiped under the big tree. I missed a cappella chants, led by one and repeated by another, beating to the sound of the drum as we worshiped underneath that tree.

Patsy preaching in small bamboo church

I missed the culture where relationships were the most important part of one's day. I missed the community, the gratitude people had for small material possessions. The box of *Good and Plenty* candy, brought to us by missionaries from our home state in the United States, for example. In Madagascar, I made the treat of tasting the familiar candy last for months, eating one a day, after lunch and sucking it over an hour's nap. In the States it seemed like I had an insatiable appetite—I was not truly satisfied with anything.

I found freedom of expression in journal writing:

> I miss Madagascar. Amazing thought, really. Here I am living at a friend's house on the Gold Coast of Florida. Wealthy USA. Million-dollar homes sit on the inter-coastal

water way. I have a boat in the back yard, accompanied by a pool and a whirlpool. And I miss living by a slum of the 9th poorest country of the world? I must ask myself the question…what do I truly miss? Do I miss the filth? The grime? The public beach used as a latrine? The poverty? The sickness? The heat?

Since my answer is *no* to all the above, I ponder more deeply. What is it that I miss about living by a slum in one of the poorest countries of the world?

I do believe it must be living in community. As much as it is an inconvenience to go outside, downstairs, and through another family's living space to get a cold glass of water from my refrigerator, it can be used as an opportunity to interact with the community. Spiritually, Madagascar is a "parched and weary land where there is no water."[96] Yet, as our body and soul long for the Lord Jesus Christ, He makes himself known to us through the blessing of community. Commune = Living together. Unity = as one unit. Living together as one unit. At peace with one another. Blessed are they that live together in unity.

This is one of the facets that developing countries have to offer the western world. Unity. Love, Peace. Patience. Enduring circumstances. They are not waiting for enhanced circumstances to enjoy life. They are not waiting for the weather to clear, or life to get easier before they learn to smell the roses. I guess they know the truth, the statement written on the back of the twenty-five foot sailboat docked next door. Carpe Diem. Seize the Day.

I ponder the vast differences of medical facilities throughout the world today. Is it a blessing or a curse to have so many medical technologies? My first thought is that it would truly be a blessing as then we know how to take care of our bodies; what might be strong, warding

---

[96] Psalm 63:1 (New Living Translation).

off disease, preventing that which might tend to otherwise come. I am keenly aware that the Malagasy don't have such a luxury. They live for the day...maintenance...daily survival and they are truly grateful when their eyes open the next morning. Somehow, they don't take life for granted. Carpe Diem. Seize the Day.

And then we have the other side of the coin. While waiting for one of our many doctor appointments last week, Todd picked up People Magazine in a waiting room, since there was no Sports Illustrated. As he opened the magazine, he began to read.

A man who was formerly a woman had a sex-change and all the male body parts were sown into place. However, they must not have removed the female reproductive system as she (or he?) was now pregnant. So here it was pictured: a woman, transformed on the outside to be a male, impregnated with a baby, and a woman at his (her?) side.

Will not this baby grow up confused, wondering, Whose am I? Where do I come from? Is my mom male or female? Who is the father/mother? How do we teach children to grow up in a world which grants any request— even sex-changes and where "males" are having babies!

I re-wrote the question in my journal.

Is medical technology a blessing or a curse? Are people more content in knowing that life is short? Fifty-six is the average life span in Madagascar. Or as people accessible to so much medical assistance in the Western World, do we want to live on and on? Is it because we are really *afraid to die?*

The current reading from Daily Forward encourages us to pray for those who heal the sick, care for the wounded, or conduct research to improve the health of humanity.[97] I am also reminded to pray that the researcher might glorify God and not necessarily come up with all the answers from a human perspective. I am further encouraged to pray the prayer found in The Book of Common Prayer:

'Direct us, O Lord, in all our doings with thy most gracious favor, and further us with thy continual help, that in all our works begun, continued and ended in Thee, we may glorify thy holy Name and finally, by thy mercy, obtain everlasting life; through Jesus Christ our Lord. Amen'[98]

Going Home

Todd was leaving to go back to Madagascar and I sat poolside on the inter-coastal waterway in a culture where neighbors didn't seem to have time to talk to one another. I penned letters to be hand-carried to my friends living in bamboo huts with an average income of seventy-five cents a day. The world is a strange place. Uneasy, I wondered how I could help change it, making things a bit more equal.

We can learn a lot from the story of Esther. She knew it would be against the law to come before the King unless he had requested her to appear. If she did not find favor in his sight, she could be killed. But once again, we find a biblical

---

[97] September 17, 2008.

[98] *The Book of Common Prayer*, 832.

story that emphasizes the willingness of a person to sacrifice her life for the sake of others.

The wisdom of Mordecai spoke to her. Her uncle, who worked at the palace, realized salvation and deliverance of the Jews would come from some place, and believed it to be to Esther's benefit to take part in God's plan. What's more, who can say but that Esther had been elevated to the palace for just that specific time and purpose?[99]

Lord, may we be willing to do the same, to be strong and confident in our call and design in this world, knowing that you have intended us for a specific purpose. Flood our hearts with your light, so that we can understand the wonderful future you have promised to those you have called. Let us realize the rich and glorious inheritance you have given to your people.[100]

An African Mindset in an American World

It's like I had an African mindset in an American world. Due to our twenty years on the mission field, I began to think more like an African, yet when I traveled to the U.S., I needed to be sensitive to the American culture.

---

[99] Esther 4:14.

[100] Ephesians 1:17-18.

I found this to be the case one night when I needed to call a family in the United States that I didn't know really well and ask if I could stay at their house, using it as a home base for ten days. I was a bit nervous and shy about calling because it isn't the American way to just invite yourself into someone's home to stay overnight, much less coming and going for ten days. Not willing to give in to insecurity or fear I made the phone call and, of course, they generously and graciously opened their home to me. It was a wonderful visit, but I reflected on the fact that by inviting myself to their home I was acting out of an African cultural mindset in an American world.

People Are Wealth

Humans adapt rapidly to luxuries they buy. The adaptation happens so rapidly that any happiness from their purchase seems relatively short-lived compared to things that produce a lasting happiness. Many Americans, in particular, tend to discount things that produce lasting happiness, such as social relationships with friends and family. Instead they buy toys and luxuries that fail to produce lasting happiness.[101]

---

[101] Nathan Davis and Beth Davis, *Rebound from Burnout: Resilience Skills for Ministers*, (Springfield: AGWN, 2010), 168.

Malagasy are known for their insightful proverbs, which are many times written on their *lambas*. As I learned from the kitchen window and porch balcony, I realized the particular truth of one specific proverb: *Ny olona no harena.* (People are wealth.) "The reality that people often wake up to is that life is a gift they have been taking for granted, and that people matter more than money."[102] I am because we are.

This is the ultimate truth of the gospel. I am because Jesus is. The Africans realize that they cannot find their identity apart from their community. It is not something they try to find independently or on their own. The same holds true for all Christians. Our identity is in Christ Jesus. We cannot separate ourselves from him. He is the vine, we are the branches, and apart from him we can do nothing.[103] I am because we are, and we are because Jesus is. When we awaken each morning that must be our starting place. Now it was time to build on what the Malagasy people had.

---

[102] Jonathan Haidt, *The Happiness Hypothesis: Finding Modern Truth in Ancient Wisdom* (New York: Basic Books, 2005), 140.

[103] John 15:5.

WHERE I, CHARESE MCGREGOR, AM FROM

I'm from a third culture, confusion, chaos, and
contradiction when talking about home.
Just the thought of it makes me quiver.
I've been to so many countries that I have to
categorize them by continent.
Birthed in the Windy City, I was whisked off to Florida
before I could barely open my eyes, where my parents
prepared to take me to foreign countries before
I even learned to walk.
I'm from a few, carefully selected toys, stuffed
inside shoes and packed into suitcases.
I'm from red dirt pathways, not fit for a stroller,
carried on a porter's back.
I'm from a multitude of languages. My first word was
omby,the Malagasy for "cow," speaking it before English.
I'm from a land of rice and *loka*,
preferring it to the macaroni and cheese packets,
hand-carried from the States.
I'm from countries where I could roam barefoot outside
and even wander in nothing but my birthday suit.
I'm from foreign cities, deserts, rainforests, and mountains,
traveling around the world before I was in kindergarten.
I'm from little electricity and occasional running water.
I'm from a family that walked village-to-village,
building relationships with Malagasy people, always on the
go, learning the system, rarely stopping to take a breath.
I'm from a dad who wanted to be with us more,
but the Lord had him evangelizing constantly,
via helicopter or ox cart, or dug-out canoe.
I'm from a mom who barters, teaches, and loves,

persuading me to walk miles without complaining
for a piece of gum.
I'm from singing, dancing, and music.
I'm from constant traveling, with no place to call home,
but a friend to call on every continent.
I'm from two different worlds:
secular and Christian, welcoming and rejecting,
imposing and accepting,
traditional and cultural.
I'm from a third culture, never knowing where
I come from, not caring where I go,
just understanding who I am.
I am because we are.

Malagasy gather as a church community
to pray for completion of The Gathering Place

Opportunities for Reflection:

Whenever we attend a baptism, we are asked to renew our own baptismal vows. "Will you . . . respect the dignity of every human being?" In answer, we pledge, "I will, with God's help."[104] Reflect on the following statements by Mother Teresa who spent her life living in community, serving the poorest of God's people in India. Record the thoughts in your journal.

"Holiness is not a matter of this or that pious practice; it consists of a disposition of the heart which makes us small and humble in the arms of God, aware of our weakness, yet confident, boldly confident in the goodness of our Father."[105]

"If we were humble, nothing would change us, neither praise nor discouragement. If someone were to criticize us, we would not feel discouraged. If someone would praise us, we also would not feel proud."[106]

"As long as we make the best effort we are capable of, we cannot feel discouraged by our failures. We cannot claim any successes either. We should give God all the credit and be extremely sincere when we do so."[107]

---

[104] *The Book of Common Prayer*, 305.

[105] Katherine Spink, *Mother Teresa: An Authorized Biography* (New York: HarperCollins, 2011) 235.

[106] Quote attributed to Mother Teresa, found on-line at http://www.inspirationpeak.com/cgibin/search.cgi?boolean=and&page=21

[107] Jose Luis Gonzales Balado, compiler, *Mother Teresa, In My Own Words* (Ligouri, MO: Liguori Publications, 1997), 35, Accessed at http://www.

How can you also have the same attitude as Christ, respecting the dignity of every human being, being the servant of all? In your journal list several ways you can exemplify servanthood to those in your life and surrounding community.

scribd.com/doc/62939845/Mother-Teresa-In-My-Own-Words (PDF Created: 12/04/2002).

TAMANA

PART SIX: BUILD ON WHAT THEY HAVE

"Will you strive for justice and peace among all people?"
"I will, with God's help."[108]

THE GUEST ROOM WINDOW

The Contractor Ran Off with Half the Money

*D*ue to circumstances beyond my control, I missed the Washington/Paris link of the return trip from the U.S. to Madagascar and was delayed two days in northern Virginia. Thankfully, when I called nearby friends, they were available and picked me up at Dulles Airport, welcoming me into their lovely

---

[108] *The Book of Common Prayer*, 305.

home. As I enjoyed the summer weather and relaxed around the pool for two days, I anticipated further adjustment. Todd sent an e-mail earlier that morning saying that The Gathering Place (bishop's residence and diocesan offices), was not completed as hoped; therefore, after several years of waiting while our planned home was under construction, we would not yet be leaving "the box" in Ankilifaly and moving into our desired abode.

Construction on The Gathering Place delayed,
awaiting the roof

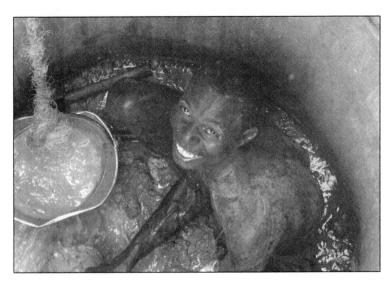

Local Malagasy digs well by hand at The Gathering Place

214

On church property with The Gathering Place, a small
bamboo church, and housing for student evangelists

We had anticipated moving onto the church property that
had been purchased not far from the Toliara airport, in a village
called Andranomena. Two years earlier an architect who flew
over from the United States pro bono had worked closely with
us to brainstorm a master plan of The Cathedral Complex that
included a bishop's residence, diocesan offices, an educational
center, dormitory, staff housing, guest housing, and cathedral.
Circumstances beyond our control continually delayed the
building of The Gathering Place. The first obstacle was that it
took two years to get the titles for the three pieces of property.
Acquiring one title in Madagascar can take months. Originally we

thought two titles were needed, but in the end it was three. The second obstacle not only delayed completion of The Gathering Place, but also presented an emotionally devastating betrayal that took all the wind out of our sails: the first contractor, a church parishioner, ran off with a hefty amount of the money.

After having waited for more than four years for the completion of the residence for the bishop and the bishop's family, I had been excited to move into this community. After all, we already had the first worship service two months earlier, even when the building did not yet have a roof! Celebrating Easter[109] with over two-hundred-twenty people gathered, Todd baptized and confirmed several people desiring to mature in their walk with Christ. With a lovely view of Table Mountain and a cool coastal breeze, the veranda would overlook the compound and we would live together in community with the student evangelists, staff, and other personnel. I would even be able to watch our visitors' planes land and take off!

Instead, we were to go back and spend more time living in cramped quarters, and I had to adjust my plans for life again. What does the Lord require of us every day, wherever we are

---

[109] Spring, 2010.

in the world? To do what is right, to love mercy, and to walk humbly with our God.[110]

When I was able to make my connections and arrived back in Madagascar a few days later, I found myself once again pleading for mercy for the Malagasy people. I recorded my dubious thoughts.

> Give this country hope, Lord God. How easy it would be to pack up and not be involved in the work here: the long distance, the hardships, unrelenting poverty, the difficult language. We could make so many excuses and pack our bags like so many others, but what would that bring? More despair, more discouragement. Instead, we have come to bring hope. Hope is in the Lord alone, not in other nations which once aided and gave financial assistance to Madagascar. Due to the political crisis, most foreign aid has been withdrawn. Our hope is not in other people. People seem to forget about the Red Island. Trust in the Lord, you people of Madagascar. God helps you and protects you. Let the hope of Madagascar be on the Lord alone. 'He will bless everyone who honors him, the great and the small alike.'[111]

---

[110] Micah 6:8.

[111] Psalm 115:13 (Good News Translation).

To Bridge the Gap between the Rich and the Poor

It made me think, *"What would we like to contribute to this world?"* Although Todd's heart ached for the poor, my heart also ached for the rich, perhaps because I saw such excess and waste in developed countries and knew the smallest amount of aid given to underdeveloped countries, when used in a righteous manner, could bring such great assistance. I saw part of my role evolving to bridge the gap between the rich and the poor.

Extremes bring challenge. How could we link people of diverse economic status in common objectives without one feeling guilty for their wealth and another ashamed of their poverty? Isn't it God who gives, and God who also takes away? Isn't it all God's money anyway?

My questions continued. How do we build on what the Malagasy already have and bridge the gap between the rich and the poor? How do we motivate the church in the United States to develop a global mindset and be involved in developing countries? How do we urge people to become people reaching people? How do we help people to globally view life through the eyes of Christ, persuading them to come out of their comfort zone, deny themselves, and take up their cross to follow Christ?

First, it is beneficial to see mission as an opportunity and a responsibility, not an obligation. It is not something we should do because we pity the less fortunate in the world. Rather, it is something we are called by Christ to do in service to him. We have the opportunity and responsibility to pray for our mission partners, support mission work financially, and travel to partnering countries to participate in mission because this is the will of God. As a result, God blesses us in order for us to be a blessing to others.

Second, mission is a privilege. God has entrusted us with his word, his good news, his gospel. What a privilege to carry it forward for others to hear and listen! This life-changing mission of transformation becomes an honor, a privilege, a responsibility—yours and mine—not a burden that weighs us down, but a God-given responsibility! If Jesus could change the world with just twelve people, imagine what he can do when each member of the body of Christ uses his or her spiritual gifts! The church of Christ is built up when individual members realize that God has created them for a specific purpose only they can fulfill.

People Reaching People

Todd and I had decided that a significant step to bridge the gap between nations was to build a support team and start a non-profit organization called People Reaching People Inc.[112] Before our first group meeting in Kinloch Farms, Virginia, September 2007, partners were brought before the Lord in prayer asking that God would instill God's dream and vision in each person, causing each one of us to use our gifts and talents to the glory of God and for the benefit of the body of Christ.

The mission statement and core values were chiseled out at the second meeting a year later: "To transform lives and make disciples of Jesus Christ by serving the poorest of the poor in Eastern Africa through economic, educational and evangelistic developments." Four core values provide the purpose of the People Reaching People community:

1) *Glorifying God*: We believe in glorifying God through worship and living in harmony with others.

2) *Transformation in Christ through relationships*: We believe in transforming lives through Christ by strengthening God's people, empowering the poorest of the poor,

---

[112] In 2007. A complete history can be seen at www.peoplereaching.org.

reaching out to and linking people through evangelism, education, and economic development.

3) *Living the Great Commission:* We believe in living the Great Commission through evangelism and discipleship, reminding God's people to be a bridge, reaching all nations with the hope of the Gospel.

4) *Christian integrity:* We believe in living transparent and obedient lives, praying that our witness will reveal holy character and a vibrant, self-sustaining ministry.

Establishment of Spiritual Gifts

We will celebrate a great day when the body of Christ is able to accomplish great things for God, when we as people reaching people gain knowledge of who we are in Christ and begin to realize our victory in Christ as children of God; then we can freely use our gifts and talents to the glory of God.

Adam didn't have to search for significance. That attribute was the result of creation. He enjoyed a sense of safety and security as all his needs were provided, and he enjoyed one-on-one communication with God and another human being, Eve. Adam had a sense of belonging. When we are comfortable and secure in who we are in Christ, we will use our gifts to the glory of God and the benefit of the church, much like a young physically handicapped evangelist who learned to ride his bicycle here in Toliara. Only because he was first given the bicycle as a gift can he now carry another person sitting on the crossbar, despite the fact that he walks with a cane. The evangelist first had to learn to ride the bike himself, spending hours adjusting balance and attempting to ride with one foot. He learned to place his cane in a strategic position so it would not inhibit his steering, but would be available for him when he stopped. I was amazed that he could ride, steer, and peddle with one leg. Imagine the surprise when I saw him riding in town a few days later, carrying someone else along with him! Likewise, when we learn to use the gifts that God has given us, we give him glory as we use these gifts for the benefit of the church and body of Christ, in spite of our own limitations.

Max Lucados' book *Cure for the Common Life*[113] talks about living in our sweet spot, finding our passion in life, and taking part in what really makes us tick. Lucado urges us to discover our STORY: **S**trengths, **T**opics, **O**ptimal Conditions, **R**elationships, and then say **Y**es!

What is the ministry God has called you to do? Lucado suggests asking three questions when deciding:

---

[113] Nashville: Thomas Nelson, 2011.

1) What work am I really good at?

2) What do other people say I am really good at?

3) What needs of people do I see?

I began applying this idea to my life in Toliara. What caused growth in an environment that was so challenging? Specifically, it was due to the grace of God. I am what I am because of the great I AM. Secondly, I have a God-given passion to spread the gospel through life-style evangelism. But how did I develop this passion? It helped me discover this when I took a look at my background.

All through childhood I loved being outside. I remember precious days in Texas, being forever outdoors, roller skating, playing with the neighborhood kids, raking leaves into a maze, imitating Julie Andrews and dramatizing the *Sound of Music* with my sister, performing shows for our parents. But I didn't like school. I didn't dislike it, but it wasn't my favorite experience in life. I didn't like being pushed into a mold. I had a passion for making the plain into something exciting. I had a zest to live life, and found it limiting to sit in a schoolroom chair bound by cement walls.

I loved playing with my stuffed animals, making them into people. And my dolls! I loved playing with my dolls. I remember inviting the nuns who lived at the retreat house down the street. Mom would offer them a break from their liturgical, rhythmic pattern of life, and they would join us for dinner and a glass of wine. And what do I remember loving about college? Socializing: being with people, leading the sorority, challenging my sorority sisters to do things differently, being the captain of the tennis team. I would much rather talk to someone than study. It wasn't that I was lazy or foolish. I just loved being with people and found myself at the library...to talk to people! As an extrovert, I love a party and a deep one-on-one conversation with a friend.

I would like to think I have an impact on people. Like a hammer in the toolbox, I can drive a point into a wall, giving people a new perspective to consider. The flip side of this trait would be driving the nail too deep, not allowing space between the nail and the structure. People need space and freedom to think and make their own decisions, so I work on presenting my point positively, not overly harsh, but at the same time, persuading people to go beyond their comfort zone, challenging them to think outside the system. As sorority president, I loved sharing my faith with those sitting on the fence, especially while attending a party. Whether or not they remembered the conversation the next morning was their decision. My responsibilities were sharing the gospel, impacting people through deep discussions and one-on-one relationships, bridging the gap in a diverse group of people, and building community.

On my first date with Todd, he asked me over a piece of pizza. "Patsy, what are your goals in life?" At the age of twenty-four I knew my answer. It was not managing the international office for professional tennis players, as I was doing at the time, but to nurture family. What was my response to the handsome man sitting across the table on our first date? "To be the best wife and mother I can be." The blunt answer might have frightened the average adult male but Todd has never been easily intimidated. Good thing. He is now married to a hammer.

God gave me the grace to do that which I had answered to the young man on our pizza date, even on the mission field in a variety of settings. Now that our children are transitioning through other seasons of life, the needs change. The needs are not as hands-on as they were when I was changing a diaper or placing a bandage on a scraped knee, but they are still there.

My role as a mother never changes. I am called to nurture and marinate our children in prayer.

I found that was another aspect of what I savored from life in Ankilifaly—marinating life in prayer. Prayer builds community and glues us together as a family. I found my gifts were not only used, but also needed in Ankilifaly. Being a hammer was helpful. The environment was hard like cement. In order to impact people I needed to pound the nail into the cement wall, balancing the gift of prophecy with the gift of nurturing. I often had to think outside the box and encourage others to do so as well. Ankilifaly needs someone to speak up, challenge the system, and help defeat the cycle of poverty. *"Will you strive for justice and peace among all people? I will, with God's help."*[114]

There is a great need for Christians to live out their calling and push on toward the upward call of Christ Jesus.[115] God, who sets us apart before we are born, calls us through his grace and is pleased to reveal his Son to us so that we might proclaim him. He is glorified in that.[116] Like the parable of the five talents,[117] God gives us gifts and desires us to use those gifts to

---

[114] *The Book of Common Prayer*, 305.

[115] Philippians 3:14.

[116] Galatians 1:11-24.

[117] Matthew 25:14-30.

build up the house of God for his glory. Let us be confident in our call, walking in the power of the resurrection.

Seder Dinner

New church traditions began. Each Holy Week a Seder dinner was given for the church leaders and student evangelists to inform and enlighten the historical Passover practices of the early church. For three and one-half hours we sat on mattresses removed from the students' beds and placed on straw mats, eating and explaining the customs of the Last Supper Jesus would have shared with his disciples during the Passover meal, commemorating God's deliverance of the Hebrews from slavery in Egypt. The Passover meal traditionally teaches us that we must all consider ourselves as slaves in Egypt, once walking in darkness. With this knowledge, we are able to fully celebrate our own deliverance.

One specific Seder dinner piggybacked the visit to the Ft. Dauphin museum and historical account of the Malagasy slaves, and I was especially attentive to the emphasis of freedom, deliverance, redemption, and thanksgiving. During the Seder meal, four cups of wine are served. Each cup focuses on one of the aspects of God giving freedom, deliverance, redemption, and finally a reason for thankfulness.

The first cup proclaims Passover as the day of freedom. God is faithful and forever fulfills his promises to those who trust in him. The inspirational liturgy includes, "In every age, oppressors rise against us to crush our spirits and bring us low. From the hands of all these tyrants and conquerors, from the power or anything that hinders us from being His people, the Lord rescues and restores us.[118]" Compassionate tears of forgiveness slid down my checks as I thought of the tyrant Flacourt who killed several Malagasy people just because he got a rise out of seeing the sight of blood, and how he captured and sold them into slavery, sending them to Reunion Island. I then thanked God for the freedom we all have in Christ and renewed my commitment to the Malagasy people to make sure I fulfill my responsibility in giving as many people as I meet the chance to know this absolute freedom.

Dipping parsley in salt water and eating bitter herbs and sweet *charoset* (apples and cinnamon) signifies life being a combination of positive and negative experiences, often a mixture of joy and sorrow. Life is even somewhat confusing at times

---

[118] Dennis Bratcher, "Introduction to a Christian Seder," *The Voice: Biblical and Theological Resources for Growing Christians*, Christian Resources Institute, http://www.cresourcei.org/seder.html.

with its bitter endings and sweet new beginnings. It is not our goal to eliminate the negative experiences and pretend that life is all sweetness and happiness. That is a futile and dishonest task. Rather our goal is to rejoice in the fact that God works in all circumstance of life, just as he heard the cries of Israelite slaves and brought deliverance.

The second cup is consumed as a symbol of celebration of the deliverance that God has brought to us. It is a privilege to praise God, thank him, rejoice in him and honor him. He brings us from bondage into freedom, sorrow into joy, slavery into redemption. When it comes to the third cup, the traditional Jewish order of the Seder now moves into the Christian celebration of the Eucharist. Finally, the fourth cup is lifted in celebration of thanksgiving and hope. We thank God for his enduring grace and love to us. The Seder then ends with reciting the Lord's Prayer. The Seder is a compelling celebration, reminding us that life is sometimes hard and filled with suffering and tears. Along with that suffering come the celebration of freedom and the wonderful deliverance that God brings us. Moving from being slaves in Egypt to the throne of grace, it's a glorious contrast.

The Seder dinner is one of the teaching tools to explain something deep within Jewish culture handed down through generations from the time the angel of the Lord passes over Egypt. The Malagasy tend to be very pragmatic, both socially and relationally. This meal allows something practical to grasp and explains why we have the Eucharist in the modern church. We were building traditions for the Malagasy people to cherish and call their own.

The Same Attitude as Christ

Grass-roots ministry can be quite exciting and exhausting at the same time. When the cornerstone for St. Gregory's Malagasy Episcopal Church in Ft. Dauphan was laid,[119] I was contemplative during the Palm Sunday processional the following day. As we held the palms above our heads, my thoughts were stirred like the branches in the breeze. I began to think how easily we accept Christ when it is to our advantage, as the people in Jerusalem hailed the King during the triumphal entry and enjoyed the Last Supper. How quickly we also deny him when it gets hard, falling asleep as on the night of Gethsemane. How willing we are to serve God in comfort, but promptly

---

[119] March 27, 2010.

deny him when he calls us to take up our cross and follow him to the hard place, or when questioned by our peers.

Philippians 2:1-11 reminds us to have the same attitude as that of Christ Jesus. When we live with the attitude of Christ, he will make us strong, comfort us with his love, bestowing upon us kindness and compassion for others. When we have the same thoughts as Christ, we share the same love and are one in soul and mind, which will bring contentment and spread happiness to this world. We need to be careful to abstain from doing anything from selfish ambition, nor from a desire to boast, but be humble toward others, considering them better than ourselves. Christ's attitude of humility allows us to be concerned for others' interests, taking the nature of a servant, walking the path of obedience all the way to his death on the cross. When we live with the same attitude as Christ, we live in his honor, falling on our knees and openly proclaiming that Jesus Christ is Lord.

Philippians 2:12 reminds us that working out our salvation is a process and takes time. "Continue to work out your salvation with fear and trembling." We are a work in progress because God is always at work in us, to make us willing and able to obey his own purpose.

My pious thoughts snapped back to reality when I heard the cock crow, three times, as if prompted by God at the opportune time during the Palm Sunday service. Maybe the meaning of "before the rooster crows[120]" represents a very common experience. In many parts of the world roaming chickens are not a rare occurrence where they crow all throughout the day and night. Jesus was making a point. Peter's denial was to come quickly and often. He knew it was coming. Even so, what was Jesus' response? His body suffered, but his spirit rested. Even though betrayed, he gave up his will for his Father's.

Agile fingers folded long, narrow palm branches into crosses, and an eighty-seven year old man was helped to kneel at the cushions placed before the bishop in order to confirm his faith along with twenty-five other faithful followers of Christ. Imagine having your first communion at eighty-seven years of age, just because you had never had the opportunity to hear the message and be taught about the goodness of God— God sent his Son Jesus into the world to die for our sins, and gives us the privilege of eternal life! Lord, send more people into the fields to reap the harvest—for the harvest is great and the laborers are few.

---

[120] Luke 22:34.

The compassion Jesus has for this world is overwhelming. He loves us to the very end; he knows our thoughts, weaknesses, and limitations. Jesus knew beforehand that, even by his own disciples, he would be betrayed. Nevertheless, he loves his people and challenges us to pray for our enemies. And what did Jesus do? He rose from the table, took off his outer garment, tied a towel around his waist and began to wash the disciples' feet. This was his extraordinary example of humility, and we are to do the same.

"If we have a faith worth living for, it's a faith worth dying for. Don't you compromise the faith that we are living and dying for."[121]

The Gathering Place

Before there were even doors, windows or a roof overhead, The Gathering Place was initiated as a place of worship. Over two hundred and twenty people gathered for Easter service, joining the seven newly baptized Christians and twelve new confirmands in Easter celebration.[122]

---

[121] Archbishop Ben Kwashi.

[122] April 5, 2010.

As I processed into the room just ahead of the bishop, I suppressed tears of joy as I scanned the room filled with people desiring to worship God. Little did I know that it would still be one month short of two years before the dedication of The Gathering Place, but I loved the fact that people were already building community and worshiping the Lord.

One of the highlights, besides celebrating Jesus as risen King, was coming with Lovely's mom, the wife of the local *shaman*. As *shaman*, her husband works hand-in-hand with the local witchdoctors and makes sure the traditional religious customs are done according to the approval of the ancestors. It was an amazing answer to prayer that she had taken up my invitation and came to church, even though her husband still did not feel comfortable enough to attend. It was delightful to see eight of Lovely's family members in the congregation. Spiritual progress was being made. Ten years ago when Lovely first came to know Jesus, she was the first of her family members to make a profession to Christ. Now, one by one, members of her entire household had come to know Christ.

Waiting

Waiting for completion of The Gathering Place was like pushing a *pousse-pousse* through a mud hole—slow, arduous, strenuous, requiring every ounce of patient energy. Life is juxtaposition. God reigns, always, everywhere. In the middle of waiting, God reigns. In the middle of selling witchcraft materials, God reigns. In the middle of unrelenting poverty, God reigns.

Patsy and construction worker standing
in front of blueprints for the Cathedral Complex

"Master, We've Worked Hard All Night and Didn't Catch a Thing"

The Gospels are filled with reminders to trust God with all our needs. "Master, we worked hard all last night and didn't catch a thing."[123] In spite of the excitement of the growth in the church and seeing many people come to faith in the Lord, discouragement rolled in like a dark cloud as we continued to the completion of long-awaited accommodations for ourselves, our staff, and students, as well as diocesan offices. My journal consisted of like prayers:

> Lord, help Todd and I to trust You to give us what we need, when we need it. We have worked hard all night. We trust You to give us strength to work, time to rest, wisdom to know what to do, finances to build The Gathering Place, educational center, dormitory, and cathedral. We also need time, energy and wisdom to write our doctoral thesis.[124]

Once again, I found reading the scriptures strengthened my inner soul and urged me to continue: "And at this time their nets were so full they began to tear!"[125] When we are obedient to God, he will give us what we need. In the Greek text

---

[123] Luke 5:5 (New Living Translation).

[124] February 10, 2010.

[125] Luke 5:6 (New Living Translation).

of this passage, Peter uses two words in addressing the Lord: "Master," representing obedience, in verse five, and "Lord," representing kingship, in verse eight. There comes a time in our own lives when we make the change from calling Jesus Master, out of obedience, to Jesus as Lord, as in kingship, the Lord being the Crowned Head of one's life.

Todd did this at a young age, when he desired to be a sports coach but decided to give his life to God's service through ministry. Out of obedience, he followed the Lord and made him his Master. His life has been an example for me to do the same.

Transformation

I wrote this from the Anglican Cathedral in Andohalo, Antananarivo:[126]

> Today is the ordination of Rev. Donne, the former village drunk who heard the gospel from Todd when he preached in the rainforest of Anosibe An'Ala several years ago. He is being ordained along with three others from the Diocese of Antananarivo. Rev. Bery preached on Luke 5, the story of Jesus calling the first disciples. Lord Jesus, hear our prayer. As Todd and I work hard for the Lord, may we catch such a large number of fish (people) that the nets

---

[126] July 25, 2010.

are about to break and we have to call in the people from the other side because of Your faithfulness. May we glorify You as we work for You, because like Simon Peter may we be aware of our sinful nature and be filled with gratitude and awe of what you have done. In Jesus' Name, Amen

I Will Bless Those Who Put Their Trust in Me

The words of Jeremiah are blunt, speaking the truth as a prophet. The Lord says:

> Cursed are those who put their trust in mere humans and turn their hearts away from the Lord. They are like stunted shrubs in the desert, with no hope for the future. They will live in the barren wilderness, on the salty flats where no one lives. But blessed are those who trust in the Lord and have made the Lord their hope and confidence. They are like trees planted along a riverbank, with roots that reach deep into the water. Such trees are not bothered by the heat or worried by long months of drought. Their leaves stay green, and they go right on producing delicious fruit.[127]

I clung to this passage to keep me steady like the anchor of a boat in a raging storm. As we awaited the official papers and creation of the new Diocese of Toliara, we asked God to give deep roots to the people in the south. We asked God to make us like trees planted along a riverbank, not bothered by

---

[127] Jeremiah 17:5-8 (New Living Translation).

heat nor worried by long months of drought. Even though we thought the creation of this new diocese would take place several years ago, and even though we still could not see the light at the end of the tunnel, we asked God to make us strong and keep us faithful. On one occasion, when we were worshiping under a litchi tree, I felt hope and envisioned the season when the tree would be ripe and ready for harvest, bearing litchi fruit which looked similar to red golf balls. Belly satisfied, we were blessed, picking and eating fruit while relaxing in the shade of the tree, savoring its sweetness.

I Prayed with the Shaman

Waiting for that harvest and waiting to move into The Gathering Place required patience. However, waiting to move allowed me to do something I had wanted to do for almost three years but had previously hesitated to do. I wanted to pray for the local *shaman*, Rivo. Like a fisherman waiting to reel in the line before the fish had bitten the hook, I had withheld, not thinking the time appropriate. Finally, I felt the Spirit of God lead, and I had the opportunity to pray with him.

After a morning walk around the city, Todd and I and one of the Ursinus College students visiting us came back from the bakery with, quite literally, our daily bread. On the way up our stairs, I stopped to talk with Lovely and Masy to arrange our next discipleship time. Lovely's father came out when we were talking and after asking how he was, he mentioned that he had a headache for several days. I asked him if he would like prayer, and for the first time, he accepted! We went back downstairs, prayed for him and a few hours later when Charese and I were walking to the market we saw him and inquired about his headache. "*Afaka!*" (Gone!) Praise be to God Almighty, and glory be to him! Two weeks later he came to church with his wife and his father-in-law! It was the first time ever he had been in a church! Because of the trust built over the years of living as the *shaman's* next door neighbor, we were finally able to pray with him.

Equipping the Saints

Prayers continued with Rivo. Right before his daughter departed to attend theological school in Kenya, we gathered outside their tin house, hands locked in a circle with her mom, dad, brothers and sisters, and friends, and prayed for a safe journey. I remembered the time Lovely came to my house upstairs, crying because her father wouldn't let her become a student evangelist. Sitting on the guest bed, we prayed that her father would change his mind, and he did! Our God reigns. He will have his way when we honor him. "Fear of the Lord teaches a person to be wise; humility precedes honor."[128]

Todd and I intentionally searched for potential leaders of the church and tapped their resources. Rivo and his wife had taught their daughter to be a woman of good character. They gave her a good upbringing, teaching her to respect her elders and family members, and instilling in her the importance of hard work and serving her community. Now that she had a personal relationship with the Lord and desired to serve God in full-time ministry, we were building on the character taught by her parents by offering her a theological education in Kenya, which would enable her to return to her Malagasy community and serve them to an even greater extent.

Reflections from the Guest Room

Transformation was occurring among the people in Ankilifaly. Perhaps it meant that we might be inconvenienced, having to go out of our comfort zone to reach those not normally on our path or in our economic bracket, but that is the

---

[128] Proverbs 15:33 (New Living Translation).

whole message of the cross. Jesus was given to us by God the Father. Because of this we now have the privilege to taking him to others.

The guest room was the relational room where I often experienced intimate conversations. It was the room where Masy cried with joy when she found out she was healed of syphilis and where I would have conversations with the massage therapist about the possibility of evil spirits. In this room I conversed with my daughters and their friends when they were home from college. It was not often that the guest room was unoccupied, but when it was empty, it would be the room in which I sat for a change of scenery offering bright light and a fresh breeze and a conversation with our house-helper Jeannette or with a friendly neighbor.

This open window didn't offer much privacy. As the room closest to the church, it was the room of hospitality. A passerby could look in, waving greetings, or English students could say hello as I smiled at them through the window. This window represented the relationships inside and out the window, focusing on others' needs, helping them to feel safe, cared for, and nurtured. It was the room in which I professed to love my neighbor as myself, taking the cross to them. The guest room was my living textbook where I was dying to myself, learning to focus my attention on others, starting with what they knew and building on what they had.

Death Is Not Always a Bad Thing

Through our journey, God will patiently have his way with us. I saw that, through my circumstances, God was breaking me down. I was dying to self. Death is not always a bad thing. It was my turn to die. "Jesus shouted out again, and he gave up his spirit."[129] In order for us to die, do we not also have to give up our spirits? I think so. We can't have the Spirit of God and the spirit of flesh working together. Like oil and vinegar, they do not mix. Something's got to give. Forgive us, Lord, for even trying.

I recorded the following in my journal:

> I'm dying, dying from self. Self is a disease that can only be cured by complete death to self. Like a cancer cell undetected in the body, the illness of self will eat away at our souls. The only remedy is Christ, and just as Christ died and rose again, we too, can live victoriously with the resurrected Christ. Alleluia. Christ has risen. The Lord has risen indeed. Alleluia!

---

[129] Matthew 27:50 (New Living Translation).

Tamana - "Happily Settled; Liking a Place or a Situation"

Although I had my moments of doubt and difficulty, I was quite surprisingly becoming at home in an environment where I never thought it possible.

What is the key to being *at home* in our hearts: comfortable, relaxed, happily settled, liking a place or a situation, enjoying the moment? Is it an expensive leather recliner or lounging at the secluded beach resort with a waiter coming to meet our every need? If this is the case, then how could I explain the harmony found living in Ankilifaly? What explained the joy I had spending hours sitting on hard benches, perspiring, learning new songs and worshiping God? What explained the contentment of those around me living in poverty-stricken Toliara?

How does the truth of the scriptures and Paul's prayer to the people in Ephesus help us to be *at home* in our hearts, wherever God places us in this world? "I pray that Christ will be more and more *at home* in your hearts as you trust in him."[130] When we meditate upon God's love and begin to grasp how deep, wide, long, and high the love of Christ really is, then he will make himself *at home* in our hearts when he is welcomed into our hearts. It's not about being at home in this world,

---

[130] Ephesians 3:17 (New Living Translation).

but rather finding our place in it. We are only guests in God's world; being *at home* is coming to the point when Christ, and his call on our lives, are finally *at home* in us!

The dreaded question for TCK's (Third Culture Kids) and missionaries, especially those who have been on the field for many years, is "Where are you from?" "Because of our deep love of family, this extreme yearning for home is considered the hardest of all to endure."[131] What is our answer? The longest I have lived anywhere in this world is Madagascar. Does that mean Madagascar was becoming home? Perhaps, but wouldn't this limit our definition of home to a physical place?

One day, as we were traveling through Asheville, North Carolina, my parents took Todd and me to the Biltmore Estate. As we drove in, the sign read "Welcome to America's largest home." The house itself was four acres in size. The only similarity to our home in Madagascar was the line of people at the gate. Could this ever be home to me? Home encompasses more than a building or a bodily place.

In reality, there are many definitions of home. It can be a place of familiarity and of special memories, perhaps, but not always, where one is known and loved. One Christmas, a

---

[131] The Northumbria Community, *Celtic Daily Prayer* (San Francisco: HarperSanFrancisco, 2002), 767.

friend gave me a beautiful lace cloth with the following words: "Home is where love grows, family is nurtured, friends are gathered." On another friend's bathroom wall was a picture with the saying, "Where we love is home. Home that our feet may leave, but not our hearts."[132] If we ask our children the definition of home, it could be, "Where we unpack." When I asked Charese this question, her response was "Home is where I sleep for the night."

When we were in the United States at a conference, we unexpectedly saw one of Todd's former students and a co-worker from northern Kenya. Rev. Kampicha hugged us tightly, grinning from ear to ear, saying, "It's like I am home now." For Africans, home is in the relationships.

But home is not always a comfortable place. Through the word of God we are encouraged to:

> Rejoice, too, when we run into problems and trials, for we know that they are good for us—they help us learn to endure. And endurance develops strength of character in us, and character strengthens our confident expectation of salvation. And this expectation will not disappoint us for we know how dearly God loves us, because he has given us the Holy Spirit to fill our hearts with his love.[133]

---

[132] Oliver Wendell Holmes, *The Poetical Works of Oliver Wendell Holmes* (Boston: Houghton Mifflin, 1975), 169.

[133] Romans 5:3-6 (New Living Translation).

Problems and trials equal strength of character and confident expectation of salvation. Expectation of salvation will not disappoint. Jesus was not in a comfortable place hanging on the cross, yet he was *at home* in this situation because he knew God's purpose was being performed as he died for us, giving up his life in sacrificial obedience and replacement for our sins. Knowledge of this truth will cause us to be *at home* in our hearts, that is, *at home* in God and Christ Jesus. Home is a place of stability.

When we were utterly helpless, Christ came at just the right time and died for us.

When we are at that point...

absolutely powerless...

the last leaf in the lettuce bag, droopy, wet,

washed out, wilted...

Christ still wants us, because He died for us.

Home is a place of dwelling...

not in a building...

but rather dwelling as Jesus did...

dwelling, among us.

Home is the presence of God residing in the center of my soul. "Lord through all the generations you have been our home."[134] While we were developing partnerships by speaking at churches in the United States one year, I picked up a bumper sticker from a local Episcopal church. It read, "You are a child of God. Come Home."[135] Don't we find truth in this definition? "All who are led by the Spirit of God are children of God."[136] It's time for us to come home to our Abba, Father, our Father God, and crawl up on the lap of our Daddy.

It's a challenge, isn't it? To come to the realization that the God we worship, the creator of heaven and earth, the one who caused Moses to part the Red Sea and turn a stick into a snake, is also the one who calls us by name. We are precious to the one who charged the galaxies, honored by the one who originated the ocean depths. His love for us is the same yesterday, today and forever.

Bishop Daddy

My daughter was in a quandary when she wanted to purchase a gift for her father's consecration as bishop. Strolling

---

[134] Psalm 90:1 (New Living Translation).

[135] Church of the Ascension, Knoxville, TN.

[136] Romans 8:14 (New Living Translation).

through the Masai market in Kenya, Corbi spotted a glass mug that could be hand engraved. That was it. She discovered the gift she wanted to give to her father. Finding the glass mug wasn't the dilemma. The difficulty was deciding on the words to engrave on the mug.

Corbi realized that her father's new-found position was one of respect and honor and wanted to acknowledge that, but she also knew that she was her daddy's precious little girl, his child. The gift was to have a dual purpose, to show her father meaningful reverence, along with being a gift of intimacy, which only a child could give. She settled on the words, "Bishop Daddy."

Abba Father

Likewise, we can have an intimate relationship with God, the creator of the universe, and call him, "Abba, Father." When we come to the realization that God's love is without measure, with no boundaries or limitations, we find our place in this world sitting at the feet of Jesus, at the throne of our God. This is when home truly becomes where the heart is. It is the core of our being. It is where we *are*. It is where we reside, where we live and move and have our being.[137] It is the center, our vortex, only found in who we are in Jesus Christ. I am because he is. Home is Christ in our heart.

Like a kaleidoscope of ever-moving glass pieces, our lives are in perpetual motion. Every falling piece of stained glass brings a varicolored picture, a multifaceted perspective, a contrasting way of viewing the world. These new representations challenge us to find new perspectives in our lives. They challenge us to be *at home* in our hearts no matter what situation arises. Home is having a heart at rest.

"At the end of the day we need a place of rest inside ourselves to return to."[138] This is returning home to the place where we find Jesus. This place of rest is the sanctuary of our inner souls, where Jesus is becoming more and more *at home* in our hearts. The priest from northern Kenya was right. Home is in the relationships. It is finding our place in this world, on the lap of our Abba, Father, and reveling in our intimate relationship with Him. Home is being in the presence of God. *Tamana* is knowing that Christ has built his home in us.

> We have gone to the people.
> We have lived among them.
> We have learned from them.

---

[137] Acts 17:28.

[138] The Northumbria Community, *Celtic Daily Prayer*, 590.

We have loved them.
We have started with what they know.
We have built on what they have.
But that, on its own, does not create a home.
Tamana is knowing that Christ has built his home in us.

WHERE WE ALL ARE FROM
(Based on Psalm 139)

We come from a God who knows everything about us.
He knows when we sit down or stand up,
he knows our every thought when far away.
He charts the path ahead of us,
and tells us where to stop and rest.
Every moment He knows where we are.
He knows what we are going to say
even before we say it!
He both precedes us and follows us.
He places His hand of blessing on our heads.

We can never escape from His spirit!
We can never get away from His presence!
If we go up to heaven, He is there;
If we go down to the place of the dead, He is there;
if we ride the wings of the morning,
if we dwell by the farthest oceans,
even there His hand will guide us,
and His strength will support us.

He made all the delicate, inner parts of our bodies
and knit us together in our mothers' wombs.
Thank you, Lord, for making us so wonderfully complex!
Your workmanship is marvelous—and how well we know it!

You watched us as we were being formed in utter seclusion,
as we were woven together in the dark of the womb.
You saw us before we were born.
Every day of our life was recorded in your book.
Every moment was laid out
before a single day had passed.

How precious are your thoughts about us, O God!
They are innumerable!
We can't even count them;
they outnumber the grains of sand!
And when we wake up in the morning,
you are still with us!

WE ARE because HE IS

Opportunities for Personal Reflection:

"It took me a number of years to realize my husband was never going to conform to my image,"[139] and the Lord was going to have his way with me. Sometime or another, I needed to surrender.

When I did, I realized that home is finding our place in this world. *Tamana* (happily settled; liking a place or situation) became a place of being established, not in a building or in a certain environment, nor from accomplishments, monetary advantage, social worth, or number of friends. *Tamana* comes from being settled in the sanctuary of the inner chamber of our hearts, which God created before we were even born. It is "the sense of being where God has called us to be, which is probably the most precious thing any believer can have."[140]

People from England use the word *settle* to describe a long wooden bench situated in front of a fire, used to enjoy a cozy conversation and a cup of tea. From this root comes the word used for American *settlers*, those who pioneered the land and found their home.

How are you finding yourself to be at the place where God has called you to be? Record your thoughts in your journal.

Find a quiet spot and allow your mind to meditate on Psalm 139, especially verse 16. "You saw me before I was born. Every day of my life was recorded in your book. Every moment was laid out before a single day had passed." How does the knowledge that God has cared for you from the very beginning of your creation affect your daily life?

---

[139] Omartian, *The Power of a Praying Wife*, 26.

[140] Williams, *Marriage, Mitres*, viii.

...the Lord who created you says: 'Do not be afraid, for I have ransomed you. I have called you by name; you are mine. When you go through deep waters and great trouble, I will be with you. When you go through rivers of difficulty, you will not drown! When you walk through the fire of oppression, you will not be burned up; the flames will not consume you. For I am the Lord, your God...you are precious to me. You are honored and I love you.'[141]

I realized my years in Ankilifaly had taken me on a pilgrimage, as life is a pilgrimage.

A pilgrimage is not a vacation; it is a transformational journey during which significant change takes place. New insights are given. Deeper understanding is attained. New and old places in the heart are visited. Blessings are received. Healing takes place. On return from the pilgrimage, life is seen with different eyes.[142]

What is your current pilgrimage? List the ways you are settling into your pilgrimage and God's call on your life. Include writing ways you are beholding life with different eyes.

---

[141] Isaiah 43:1-4 (New Living Translation).

[142] Sister Macrina Wiederkehr, O.S.B., *Catholic Digest*, April 2000, 88.

EPILOGUE

*A*fter twenty plus years of following my husband on the mission field, there is a time for me to lead. In August 2012, at the invitation of The Most Reverend Ian Ernest, Archbishop of the Indian Ocean and also Bishop of the Diocese of Mauritius, I packed my suitcases and went to Mauritius, leaving my husband for one year to cope with his miter in Toliara, Madagascar. My assignment is to lead a church, St. Simon the Fisherman, in Tamarin, Mauritius. I am shepherd of a flock and a pioneer for women's ordination as the first woman priest working in the Anglican Diocese of Mauritius. I also will be mentoring women in discernment and on the path to ordained ministry in the diocese.

Being fully empowered and authorized to exercise all my gifts in ordained ministry has caused me to come alive. Like a freshly watered plant, quenched after years of drought, I have been saturated in my passion of nurturing souls and providing nourishment and strength to enable them to glorify God in this life and in the life to come.

I did not fully realize my working in Mauritius would have such an impact on the church, the country, or me in general. I was just once again being obedient, counting it a blessing from the Lord to have a year break from the poverty and hardship in Madagascar and instead working in a tropical paradise. In his 1897 equatorial visit to Mauritius, Mark Twain was quoted as stating, "Mauritius was made first, then heaven."

History pages were turned for the church on September 23, 2012, at my Induction Service as the first woman priest to serve as priest in the Anglican Diocese of Mauritius. Segments of the service and a personal interview were televised on national TV. Interviews with several different papers took place and my picture appeared in papers and even on the front page of a magazine. The Vicar General of the Catholic Church, when questioned about women's ordination, said there is no "doctrinal, theological or biblical reason that women should not be allowed to become priests." *L'Express*, the national newspaper, also included an article on the leadership of women in other religious traditions, including Islam and Hinduism.

A new day is dawning. The follower has become a leader. I am to live into the calling I have received (Eph 4:1) and God is going to guide my path.

Ecclesiastes 3:1 reminds us that, "There is a time for everything, and a season for every activity under heaven."

This is my time to dance.

The Reverend Dr. Patsy McGregor

December 2011, Patsy and Todd moved into the Gathering Place, which was still not completed. Construction continued for another 2 months, and it was finally dedicated March 2012

May 2012, Todd, Patsy, Charese, Corbi, and Joe (Corbi's husband) on the occasion of Charese's graduation from Ursinus College

APPENDIX
SELECTED EVENTS
February 2006-February 2013

2006

Feb The Province of Indian Ocean approved the election for an Assistant Bishop of Antananarivo and Area Bishop of Toliara with the purpose of creating a new Diocese of Toliara

July Todd: Asked to consider going back to Madagascar by Dr. Zoe

Aug Todd: Elected as Assistant Bishop of Antananarivo, Area Bishop of Toliara by the Standing Committee of the diocese

Oct The Province of Indian Ocean approved Diocese of Toliara

Sept 3 Patsy: ordained to priesthood, All Saints Diocese, Anglican Church of Kenya

Dec 10   Todd: Consecrated as Assistant Bishop of Antananarivo, Bishop of Toliara, at St. Laurent Cathedral, Antananarivo, Madagascar. McGregor family returns to Kenya for the Christmas season

2007

Jan 14   Todd: Installed as Area Bishop of Toliara, Eklesia Episkopaly Malagasy, at the Roman Catholic Theatre, Toliara (church not yet complete in Ankilifaly) Todd remained in Toliara and Patsy returned to Kenya/ USA and returned to Toliara in November 2007

June   Todd and Patsy: First residency, Doctoral Program in Outreach and Discipleship: Gordon Conwell Theological Seminary, Charlotte, NC

July   Patsy and Todd attend Corbi's graduation, Rift Valley Academy, Kijabe, Kenya

Aug   Corbi: First year, Dickinson College, Carlisle, PA Charese: Final year at RVA, Kijabe, Kenya

Sept   People Reaching People: Initial Meeting, Kinloch Farms, VA

Oct   Final shipping of family belongings to Madacascar

Nov   Charese and Patsy travel to Toliara together

Dec   People Reaching People: Vision for The Cathedral
        Complex
        Team Visit: Phil Johnson, Randy Degler, Phil
        Crannel
        First family Christmas in Ankilifaly

2008

Jan   Corbi travels back to USA and Charese returns to
        Kenya
        Evangelism Training Year 1 begins in Toliara with 5
        Malagasy students admitted

Mar   Team Visit: Downline Ministry from Memphis, TN

June   Todd and Patsy: Second residency for Doctoral of
        Ministry Program, Charlotte, NC

July   Todd & Patsy travel to Kenya for Charese's gradua-
        tion from RVA
        Todd & Patsy travel to Lambeth Conference,
        Canterbury, England

Aug   People Reaching People: Second Annual Meeting:
        Kinloch Farms, VA
        Charese begins first year at Ursinus College,
        Collegeville, PA and Corbi returns to Dickinson

Nov   Patsy's sister leads a mission team visit with students from Boca Raton Christian School

Dec   Corbi and Charese home for second Christmas in Ankilifaly

2009

Jan   Corbi & Charese: Back to school in USA

Political uprising begins in Madagascar

Evangelism Training Year 2, with 4 new students admitted

Mar   Military coup in Madagascar. Opposition takes over

Apr   People Reaching People Board Members visit Madagascar

June   Todd & Patsy: Third residency, Gordon Conwell Theological Seminary, Boston, MA

July   Will and Cheryl Harman lead team mission visit

Aug   The Rev. and Mrs. William Roberts undertake mission to build sister church: St. Gregory's Malagasy Episcopal Church in Ft. Dauphin

Sept   People Reaching People Board President Syd Verinder re-visits Madagascar

Nov   People Reaching People: Third Annual Meeting, Delray Beach, FL

Dec   Team Visits: Ed McNamara, Diocese of Albany,
        USA

        Third family Christmas in Ankilifaly with Charese,
        Corbi, and Joe who marries Corbi in July 2011

2010

Jan   Evangelism Training Year 3, with 9 students
        admitted

        Second Team Visit: Downline Ministries

Apr   Easter: First Service in The Gathering Place;
        Baptism & Confirmation service

        Todd and Patsy: Travel to USA for SAMS Retreat
        and New Wineskins

July   Teams from St. David's Episcopal Church, Glenview,
        IL and St. Mark's Episcopal Church Geneva, IL.
        St. Mark's team builds sister church St. Michael's
        Malagasy Episcopal Church

        Team Visit: Ursinus/Elon College students

Aug   Malagasy student evangelist begins seminary study
        at St. Paul's University, Kenya

        Team Visits: People Reaching People Board
        Members Syd and Laura Verinder; Howard and Peg

Hess lead a team from Church of the Ascension, Knoxville, TN;

Todd: Travel to Uganda for All African Bishop's Meeting; Congo for Evangelistic Mission in preparation for Capetown 2010

Sept   Patsy's parents, Gerry and Audrey Cox, visit Toliara Companion Diocese of Southeast Florida Medical Mission team visits Madagascar

Oct   Todd attends Lausanne Conference, Cape Town 2010

Nov   Todd and Patsy: Defend Doctoral Thesis, Boston, MA

People Reaching People: Fourth Annual Meeting, Delray Beach, FL

Dec   Fourth family Christmas in Ankililaly with Charese and Corbi

2011

Jan   Corbi and Charese return to university studies in USA

Fourth Evangelism Training with 4 new students admitted

Mar	I Want To Learn English Team visits from Florida and sets up computer lab in Ankilifaly
Apr	People Reaching People Board member John and wife Jane Griffin lead medical mission from England
May	Patsy and Todd receive D.Min diplomas from Gordon Conwell Theological Seminary
	Corbi graduates with a BS in Neuroscience from Dickinson College
July	Corbi McGregor marries Joe Sandoe
	Student from Emory University in Atlanta, GA visits
Aug	Missionary Ryan Brazille in ministry for 9 months
	Team visits from Companion Diocese of Canterbury in England
Nov	Fifth Annual Meeting for People Reaching People in Chicago, IL
	International Rooted in Jesus Team visits
Dec	Teacher from St. Andrews School in Boca Raton, FL visits Madagascar
	Todd and Patsy move into still uncompleted Gathering Place and celebrate Christmas in their new home with Charese.

2012

Jan	Charese: Back to school in USA
	Evangelism Training Year 5, with 7 new students admitted. As of 2012, 8 students in this program have been commissioned as evangelists, 2 await commissioning, 6 have had further studies, 2 have been ordained, and 6 continue in the training program.
Mar	Third Team Visit: Downline Ministries
	Gathering Place dedicated
May	Charese graduates with BA in International Relations from Ursinus College
June	Hosted family from Diocese of Albany at the Gathering Place
Aug	Patsy called by the Archbishop of the Indian Ocean as Rector of St. Simon the Fisherman Anglican Church in Tamarin, Mauritius
Sept	Patsy inducted as first woman priest in the Anglican Diocese of Mauritius
	Church member from St. Mark's Geneva, IL, attends dedication for sister church in Motombe, Madagascar
Dec	Patsy's parents spend Christmas with Patsy in Mauritius and Todd joins them to celebrate the New Year.

2013

The new Diocese of Toliara is created. Todd elected as the Diocese's first bishop on February 9. Official installation set for April 21, 2013

CPSIA information can be obtained at www.ICGtesting.com
Printed in the USA
LVOW130611210513

334679LV00001B/1/P